Tapestry

Tapestry

Barbara Young

Shoreline

Photographs from the collection of the author
Cover Tapestry design, Mouna Shawa and Barbara Young
Graphic design, Sarah Robinson

Shoreline
23 Ste-Anne, Ste-Anne-de-Bellevue, QC H9X 1L1
514.457.5733 shoreline@videotron.ca
www.shorelinepress.ca

Printed in Canada by Transcontinental Métrolitho

Dépôt légal: Library and Archives Canada
and Bibliothèque et Archives nationales du Québec

Library and Archives Canada Catalogue in Publication

Young, Barbara, 1931-
Tapestry / Barbara Robertson Young.
ISBN 978-1-896754-67-3

1. Young, Barbara, 1931-. 2. Robertson family.

3. Pointe-Claire (Quebec)--Biography. I. Title.

FC2949.P63Z48 2009 971.4'27 C2009-903969-9

Contents

Dedication

To Joanne, who always believed my work had value.

Her many friends will remember with me her kindness, her sense of justice, her wry humour, her intelligence, and her extraordinary courage.

Introduction

It was a friend's casual remark that started me on this project.

"A lot of your relatives seem to like writing," she had said, and I checked through my files to see if she was right. She was.

As I read and re-read the pieces, I realized their reminiscences, stories and poems wove a unique and colourful tapestry of family words.

Mary

Everyone is asleep. It is early morning and while waiting for the water to heat up for my morning transfusion, I'm sitting at the dining-room table writing in my journal.

As I glance out the patio door, I can see the weather is overcast. The snow that had fallen two nights ago seems water sodden, thanks to rain or thaw or both. Yesterday it was cold enough to snow and we had a few flakes overnight. It reminds me of Christmas Eve last Wednesday – so quiet, cold and peaceful, with the snow flakes wafting down gently, dusting everything with a light powder. It was so pretty.

I popped into the library earlier in the week, pleading with the librarian for a book on overcoming obstacles – city folk moving to the country and coping. We were not successful, given the short notice. I had arrived thirty minutes before closing while she was conducting a book search on Oriental fiction for another person. I ended up with a couple of books on Christmas and Mrs. Simcoe's diary.

I was intrigued by Mrs. Simcoe's Diary. Its manuscript was discovered by a Mr. John Ross Robertson (1841-1914) who published his version in 1911. It was then reprinted for the Centennial of the City of Toronto in 1934. The edition I picked up was edited by Mary Quale Innis.

When I first opened up the book to glance through it, I immediately saw the name Pointe Claire – a good omen! June 23, 1792. Further into the text, on July 31, 1796, Mrs. Simcoe related that looking at the scenery from Isle aux Soeurs "to the N. West looking over the immense width of the St. Lawrence is seen Isle aux Paix, Isle Perrot and Pointe Claire – in the distance Lac des Deux Montagnes."

"Immense width of the St. Lawrence" - that's our Lake St. Louis, obviously not yet named as such!

Even in 1792 Mrs. Simcoe wrote of the junction between the Ottawa and the St. Lawrence rivers, the Ottawa being dirt coloured and the St. Lawrence transparent.

I was amused at one comment she made that the sense of distance is of necessity different here … with the vast expanse of land … five to six hundred miles is not more considered by an American than moving to the next parish by an Englishman.

Diaries and drawn sketches help us to see what the new world was like for her:

"She resembles the lady settlers of a generation later – Mrs. Traill, Mrs. Moodie and Mrs. Stewart, in her keen interest in plants and knowledge of them though she was most unlike those ladies in her commanding social position and her prosperity."

Mrs. Simcoe tells of an interesting style of real estate transaction on Portland Island: "The inhabitants of the island have laws and regulations peculiar to themselves: for instance, the sale of land is affected by the presentation of a stick before witnesses, no writings or Parchment used and no lawyers consulted." Sept. 19, 1791.

The source of many a lawyer's headache in the future I think!

It seems we owe a debt to Robertson who collected historical material related to Toronto and the Simcoes. Text of the diary in manuscript differed from text presented to the public in 1911 under his editing. However, he salvaged huge quantities of material that would otherwise have been dispersed and lost.

I found it interesting to see the evolution of her descriptions of her life – thanks to the proliferation of letters sent to family and to a Mrs. Hunt who was caring for the Simcoe daughters who did not accompany Simcoe to Canada. The Ontario Archives holds the manuscript of the diary itself, some letters, notebooks, sketches, and two diaries, little notebooks, pruned and expanded in the final diary.

All this about Mrs. John Graves Simcoe and my primary question is … who was Mrs. Stewart … as in Stewart Hall in Pointe Claire?

It's getting unpleasant outside – damp and cold – a darker day. We will be finishing up packing the boat away for the season. The boat has been out of the water since October but we need to wrap it using a tarpaulin as a tent to protect it from the heavy snowfall. The A frame is a reasonable design, though the boys need to shore up the triangle to keep it secure by reinforcing the cross members. While we were helping move the canoe up the hill to the garage, dismantle the picnic table and its umbrella, the wind started to pick up on the lake.

As we wrapped the boat in its Christmas wrapping, the wind chill nipped at our eyes and noses. Our hands stiffened as the chill permeated the work area. Re-entering the cottage, we grabbed our handkerchiefs to stem the runny noses as our faces thawed. Necessity may be the mother of invention – cold is the mother of efficiency and ingenuity!

I am now sitting at the dining room table at about 3 p.m. gazing over the balcony towards the lake. There is a bowl of wooden fruits on the table. I wonder where that design element came from?

Mary

It's another cloudy, overcast, grey day. Looks colder than yesterday morning when the droplets of moisture hung like beading along the balcony railing. Today no beading. On the balcony floor, I can see textured patterns where the water has been frozen from the melting snow from yesterday. Jack Frost had not put his artistry on the window panes. The birds are active at the bird feeders – the blue jays are bullying and chasing off the chickadees and finches. I see a yellow and black one with a bright yellow beak. Two sets of two feeders are located within viewing distance from the kitchen window … adds a bit of entertainment as we take care of mundane duties at the sink.

I stopped into the library on my way to the historical society meeting. The weather looked stormy as the winds were whipping the snow across the road surface. The books I had requested had come in … to my delight.

I am reminded of how much I do enjoy books and reading. As refreshment, I took out a couple of the Herriot vet books … easy reading with gentle humour and a strong sense of continuity through periods of considerable change.

I also borrowed a book entitled "Remembering the Farm" by Allan Anderson. The book is subtitled Memories of Farming, Ranching and Rural Life in Canada Past and Present. This was a real gem.

Mr. Anderson's description of farm houses makes me think of the Daoust's house in Beaconsfield … entering to get to the kitchen, maybe a sun porch then a pantry room. I remember a big table, a side board, a room with African violets and windows with small panes of glass … the house reminded me of an onion … so many layers a visit was not a static thing, it was an adventure, a process.

Mary

Even though we live at the edge of a small community, it is basically rural. The cornfield is four or five houses down the road. The horse farm is across the street past three houses and a small stretch of trees … you have to pass the corn field and the horse farm to get to the elementary school. I guess that's rural, though some neighbours insist we live "in town".

In the winter the quiet can be deafening … but it is almost spiritual … sometimes I get a sense of a continuity … part past, present and future … almost timeless … very reminiscent of meditation … when I pause to absorb the moment.

It was Allan Anderson's opinion that the vastness of the country made for a qualitative difference in the Canadian farm experience. The climate also added an extra measure of toughness. A greater degree of loneliness perhaps made children more contemplative and self-reliant.

Sturdiness, a certain amount of eccentricity and even crankiness, and a strong sense of the need to do it yourself.

Katie had that resilience too … sturdiness.

This makes me think back to Wendy from Sutton whose grandmother had crossed the country into the Townships overland from the States as a young bride, carrying her valuables through the rough country. Wendy and her family struck me as people who carry on with dignity through adversity. That is a lesson I deeply appreciate, of which I should remind myself more often … The courage to follow a path not often taken … the pride of having done so … the faith to pursue it further.

Dorothy

On Christmas Eve in the year 18— the home of John Watt was a place bubbling over with happiness and thanksgiving. For the first time in several weeks 'Papa' was home from the war and besides, wasn't it Christmas? What a lovely picture the cabin made, smoke curling from the chimney, behind the tall Scotch fir trees, and, everywhere, the snow.

Inside, Martha, the mother, was putting the little tots in bed. With a beaming face she kissed them and pulled across the curtain which divided the cabin in two parts, sleeping quarters and living quarters. Over in a corner Papa Watt was putting the finishing touches on a little wagon for baby, and a smirking rag doll for Margy.

With many chuckles and hand squeezes the father and mother filled two tiny stockings with sticky taffy, apples, and nuts. Then they exchanged gifts. There was a fine, woolen muffler for John, and for Martha, a pair of beautiful gauntlets.

In the midst of this happiness came a trampling of feet and a hasty rap on the door. John went to the door, opened it and stepped out. A hasty murmuring followed and he returned. Martha, all the joy gone from her eyes, was standing by the table with a very white face. John looked at her and tried to speak. At last he whispered, "I have to go, sweet, it is my duty." Then bravely trying to smile they prepared for his leave-taking.

Soon, oh, so soon, everything was ready. After kissing his babies and smoothing his wife's hair John snatched his rifle from the wall and . . . was gone. Martha sank into a chair and buried her head in her apron. The ranks of marching men passed the little cabin and disappeared round a bend in the road.

When morning dawned the weary men were preparing for a battle. John however, was quicker than the others and sat down with his back to a tree and, smoking his pipe, thought of the two little ones and his wife at home waiting for him. Suddenly a crackling of rifle fire broke out and John's face hardened as he sprang to protect his country for Martha, and Margy, and baby.

Soon all was over; the colonists had won the battle. But John, John lay half-buried in the snow, dead.

Miles away in the cozy cabin a woman with anxious eyes watched from the window, the road by which her husband should return. Baby on the floor gurgled over his little wagon and Margy crooned a soft little song to her new treasure. As they waited, night fell.

Frederick

40 Cavell Avenue
Mimico, Ontario
June 17, 1950

Mrs. Bessie Roberston,
921 St. Clair Avenue West,
Toronto, Ontario

Dear Sister Bessie:

Please find enclosed copy of summary of origin and genealogy, the name of "Melhuish", which I mentioned would be sent you, when last I saw you.

I trust this may be of some interest to you. Hope you are keeping well as are Ross & Thalia and their respective families.

With love,

Fred & Laura Melhuish

Mr. Melhuish

The following Extracts are taken from the Dorchester & Sherborne Journal for the 18th of November 1808.

From Suddon House (a mile West of Wincanton) Mr. Melhuish gives the following particulars of the Storm there and in that Neighbourhood:

> "I observed, says this Gentleman, the Storm about six o'clock P.M. coming from the S.W.
>
> "The evening set in unusually dark for the Season of the Year, a servant of mine, who was unloading Hay near the House, was struck violently on the Arm by a Hailstone, which surprised us all, as we had not at that Time conjected what was near us. About a Minute after I discovered two or three Hailstones about the size of a Pidgeons Egg. In a few Minutes after one of the larger Dimensions fell by my side with such velocity that striking on the ground it dashed to Pieces and the different Fragments rebounded as high as my Head, in about seven or eight minutes more the Hail descended in one dreadful Storm fraught with Destruction.
>
> "In the N.W. side of the House, sixty panes of Glass were broken. Apples sufficient to make forty hogs heads of Cider destroyed, seven Acres of Oats and the unmown Grass Beaten down as flat as if a heavy Roller had repeatedly passed over it one way. The impression of the Hail on the ground was as though the Head of an Iron Bar had been forced upon it."

Thomas

This delightful description of a visit by Dr. Thomas Bartow to Crediton was included with a collection of family information gathered by Dr. Evelyn Bartow in the late 1800's.

> "Crediton is an ancient market town, situated between two hills, on the banks of the river Creedy, and divided into two parts, called the East and West towns. During the times of the Saxons it was the see of a bishop and a place of great importance, but in 1040 the see was removed to Exeter.
>
> "I visited Crediton in the year 1871, reaching the town at 4:29 p.m., June 29. I took a look at the church, strolled around the graveyard, found the tombstone and called on the vicar, who promised to show me the records the next day after morning service. Afterwards I saw the handsome new schools, the free grammar school, founded in the sixteenth century, and other objects of interest. The following day, Friday, June 30, I attended matins in the Church of the Holy Cross, which were said in the Lady Chapel by the vicar. The church is a spacious structure in the later Gothic style, built in the fifteenth century. It consists of a nave and two aisles, with a tower 100 feet high, rising from a semicircular arch in the centre of the building."

Ian

I took a break, jumped into the car, and headed southwest. Some four hours later I was in Tedburn St. Mary. Not much of a town, again a cluster of houses, two pubs, a general store and up a side street, a portacabin post office. Everything very tidy, though.

Devon appears well off with good tourist income to supplement farming. The lady in the general store said no one has written any history, there wasn't even a post card and she summed up the town as "nice but boring."

Lunch in the Kings Arms – there seems to be one in almost every town – revealed only that the village was the first refreshment stop on the road west from Exeter. Charles II is supposed to have stopped there, hence the name of the pub. Now the A30 passes north of the town and not many people leave it to stop at the pub.

I finally found the house after having driven about a mile up a rutted stone road only to find it didn't go to Melhuish Bartow Manor any more, and I had to retrace after being given directions by a 'healthy' blond wife of the farmyard I ended up in. Back through Tedburn, under the A30 on a good paved road, and there I was.

The lady of the house explained that she and her husband are tenant farmers (13 years) and that M.B.M. is part of the Fulford Estate. On the Ordnance Survey map you can see south of M.B.M. is Great Fulford, the present manor house of the estate … She knew the house was old – some of the walls are of 'cob' held together by some kind of clay or medieval cement. This is all covered today by a smooth cement rendering, but here and there it had broken away to reveal the cob. There were some very old stone things like a wash basin.

As I came away after taking photos I could see the parish church across the valley rather outside the village of Tedburn. So I went over there to photo. From it you can see M.B.M. across the valley about a mile. Lovely scenery.

Next day – off I went back to Tedburn with the idea I would trace the route of the migrating Melhuish family to Crediton, Tiverton and on up route A396 to Brompton Regis where our family line can be traced to.

The so-called road from Tedburn was paved, but so narrow it could just take the Mercedes on each side. Almost all the way were hedge rows, fortunately recently trimmed, standing on mud banks to a combined height of some eight feet or more. It seems the road was dug into the landscape because the mud banks are not much above the level of surrounding fields. Guess this is normal – but gives an idea of the age of the road. This route was "up hill and down dale." At the top of each rise one would have a fantastic view ahead of rolling hills of parched light brown fields, separated by still green hedges, and here and there an occasional clump of trees. Oak normally. Then down, down, into almost a solid tunnel of trees and bushes, quite dark, and then up again.

Still raining, lightly but steadily.

David

Beauty

The beauty is in the trees,
In the trees of the fall.

In the rushing water
Of the stream.

The birds can be heard
Singing their favorite song.

A distant school bell
Can be heard.

Cyclists cycle
On the newly paved roads ....

How life can be so
Beautiful!

Ian

I became curious about the conditions prevailing in the first half of the 19th century when our ancestor lived his short life in Somerset, so I browsed through some library books. *Nineteenth Century Britain 1815-1914* by Anthony Wood, *Historical Geography of England Before 1800*, edited by H.C. Darby and *The Age of Reform 1815-1870* by Sir Llewellyn Woodward, and made some notes.

The Battle of Waterloo, June 18th, 1815, where Wellington routed Napoleon, ended 22 years of war between Britain and France, and began a hundred years of extraordinary change in Britain – industrially, politically, socially, and economically.

At 1815 the landed aristocracy was still the head of society and the control of national and local government lay almost entirely with them. At the same time, the beginning of the industrial revolution, featuring great expansion of cotton cloth and iron production was already well established by 1800. Before that the mainly agrarian economy afforded only slow growth in population and quality of life.

At the beginning of the 18th century, three quarters of children born had died before the age of 6. The population in England and Wales in 1700 was less than 6 million, but rose to 9 million by 1801, most of that rise after 1740. Whatever other factors contributed to this – the plague had faded away, and there were more hospitals – the limit to population is the food supply, and in the course of the 18th century there was large increase in agricultural output. This would result in both a higher birth rate and lower death rate through better nourishment.

Best information is that the key crop of corn rose from 43 million hectoliters in 1700 to 61 million by 1800, numbers of sheep more than doubled and their weight individually tripled. After about 1750 corn prices began to rise and the increased labour force limited increase in wages – hence a better profit for farmers and incentive to invest in more intense cultivation through new techniques, and the greatest part of the century's increase in production occurred in the second half.

The scientific interest in farming changed the face of England, by promoting the creation of separate fields, where these did not already exist, separated by hedgerows, for grazing the farmers own livestock and experiment with new crops and methods. About 6 million acres, including 2.5 million acres of 'common' land were enclosed, mostly after 1793 when the war with France began to lift prices of agricultural produce especially high.

N.B. However, only 3.5% of land in Somerset was newly 'enclosed' compared to over 50% in counties of mid-England where it had been normal for small farmers to use pieces of large tracts of open land.

Inevitably this worked in favour of the richer farmers – the poor could not afford the cost of enclosure or even make good their claim to strips of land they had farmed and suffered virtual expropriation, leading to some drift of people to towns and cities where they supplied the expanding industrial workforce. However, a great many small farmers did remain on the land and until 1815 at least, could benefit from higher food prices. Cottagers did less well, but a few managed to pick up a small plot during partitioning of the open fields, others found a reasonable level of employment opportunity – at least until the increase in rural population began to create a surplus of labour.

The end of war in 1815 brought change, corn price was about £1.82 per hectoliter in 1813, an average of £1.24 in 1814, and by Jan 1815 had fallen to £0.87, the general level of pre-war prices. But farming costs, including taxes and interest on loans for enclosure led to many bankruptcies among farmers. Some 4/5 of the local tax was for poor relief and rising unemployment swelled by demobilized servicemen after the war pushed parish taxes upward. Labour wages fell from eighteen shillings a week to an average of 10 shillings by 1830. Corn prices continued to fall until 1835 when they reached £0.66 per hectoliter. Notably livestock farmers in the north and west suffered far less.

By the end of the 18th century some 3/4 of the cultivable land was owned by great magnates, but in the main they did not run their estates themselves, apart from a home farm to meet their own needs. The rest was usually let out to tenants and the majority of these small holdings were less than 100 acres. About 2/3 of the agricultural population were labourers. During the war with France their wages did not keep pace with the rise in prices, and a bad harvest could easily threaten them with starvation. Rabbits, hares and pheasants were abundant but it was illegal to kill game without a license. By the Gilbert Act of 1782 able-bodied poor were not sent to the workhouse, but were to be given work by the parish. The Roundsman system meant that the labourer went the rounds of the parish, where the farmers were forced to employ him, although the bulk of his wages was paid out of the poor tax. So the farmer preferentially employed lower cost poor, and men were driven to become dependent upon the parish before they could get employment.

Even after the Reform Act of 1832, the landed interest still predominated in the Government.

There were some improvements in agriculture in the 1840's but the main agrarian revolution came in the 1850's and 1860's.

From 1831 to 1851 the population increased from 16 to 20 million – with little impact in the country (mainly in cities and towns!) The Census of 1851 showed 1,800,000 men and women whose livelihood depended on the land. In 1851 agricultural labourers numbered over a million (out of 20 million total population!). Usually they were hired by the week or the day! And their standard of living depended largely upon the season or the part of the country where they lived. There were in addition some 364,000 farm servants whose position was more secure since they were hired for the year at the annual "mop" fair and lived as part of the farmer's household.

In the south, wages were as low as 42 pence per week and the labourer was often vitally dependent on what he could grow in his own garden or allotment, or on what he could poach, if he was prepared to risk the sentence of transportation (to Australia!) that the hated game laws would impose for a third offence.

By 1834, good harvest had brought the price of corn down to £.77 per hectoliter, then a bank crisis, coupled with bad harvest in 1837 and 1838 produced the most acute period of economic distress in these decades.

The one thing on which economic historians of the 19th century are agreed is that the level of life for a large part of the population was wretchedly arduous and bleak, and when a low point was reached as in the period of 1838-42, it was hardly surprising that the upper classes feared revolution.

The town of Exeter (Isca Domnoniorum) was the western terminus of the Roman road system. There are some evidences of a Roman presence in Cornwall but few on the western side of the river Exe.

By the end of the 1820's a few railway lines had been built and change from horse-drawn to steam locomotives was under way. A map of the railway system as of 1847 shows a line from Bristol to Exeter as the most western.

The education of children varied greatly according to class. There were no state schools of any kind, but in the first half of the 18th century a large number of charity schools were founded. In 1818, some 650,000 children were being educated at 18,000 endowed and non-endowed schools in England. Nevertheless, illiteracy was widespread.

There is no escaping the fact that the Church of England offered a comfortable position for many of the upper sections of society and by the end of the 18th century it had little contact with the growing numbers of urban poor.

Possibly in reaction to this lukewarm established church that two revivalist bodies emerged in the latter part of the 18th century. Methodism eventually became an independent organization – not the intention of its founder John Wesley, but the Church of England bishops refused to ordain ministers and forced a break in 1783. The numbers of Wesleyan Methodists increased from 72,000 to 231,000 in 1813.

In the latter part of the 18th century some of the Puritan sects – Presbyterians, Baptists, Congregationalists, Quakers, etc., became infected with a new enthusiasm.

In 1812 a Baptist Union for England was formed, and in 1830 the Congregationalists included 1/5 of the population and their places of worship greatly outnumbered those of the Anglican Church.

Of the many non-Conformist sects in England and Wales the largest was the Methodists whose numbers had grown from 72,000 in 1781 to 358,000 in 1850, plus another 130,000 specialist quasi Methodist groups.

The rapid growth of industrial towns and cities in the 18th century led to tightly packed, filthy slums where there was little air or light, no drainage and no pure water supply. Among the poor, typhus, typhoid, tuberculosis, smallpox, and scarlet fever were almost always present. The death rate in cities continued to increase through the 18th and to the mid 19th century. Then came cholera which first struck Britain in 1832 with 18,000 deaths. In the summers of 1848 and 1849 it raged in the cities of England and Wales and claimed more than 72,000 people. The epidemic returned in 1853 but by then efforts to clean up sanitation showed results with sharp falls in the death rate in some areas.

The development of British agriculture, industry, and commerce both within and outside the Empire produced many changes on the map as Daniel Dafoe wrote in 1724.

Dafoe found Somerset a populous and flourishing county, conditions attributable in large measure to its textile industry and its sea port towns. The county was primarily engaged in dairy farming and cheddar cheese had won for itself a high reputation.

Some 60% of the county consisted in 1797 of meadow and pasture land, and Somerset produced insufficient grain for its own consumption.

Despite its populousness and despite its industrial activity, Devonshire stood amongst the most backward agricultural regions of England.

In the West Country the localization of the various branches of the manufacture (of wool) was related above all to the availability of water supplies and of water power.

"Many people thought that subsidies paid out of the rates (taxes) to agricultural labourers encouraged improvident marriages and large families."

"In any case, high prices and bad harvests during some of the war years made the period before 1815 dismal for the poor. The diet of most labouring families was bread (wheaten bread: barley, oats, and rye had almost ceased to be used for bread before 1815) and cheese for six out of seven days of the week, although some labourers kept a pig, and many had small gardens."

Religion offered no way of escape for the majority. The very poor had not good enough clothes for attendance at church or chapel. The technique of elementary education was almost unknown – as late as 1839, 33.7% of men and 49.5% of women married in church could not sign their names in the marriage register.

The French Revolution of 1830 affected the situation: the fall of Charles X caused considerable excitement in England and brought about a revival of interest in parliamentary reform. During the autumn of 1830 troubles broke out again in the agricultural districts of southern England. Nine were hanged, 450 others were sentenced to transportation. In many cases farmers agreed to a rise in wages.

David

Longone

The sunken wrecks
Of the nine-teen hundreds.

The longone war
Is still in memory of the old ones.

The red poppies grew
On the brave soldiers' graves.

These are memories that will
Never be forgotten....

As the time goes on,
The memorial will, too.

Dorothy

It was one of the darkest days of the war period. A dreary succession of lost battles and retreats had robbed the allied nations of almost all hope of winning the war.

In our drowsy, old town there was just one refuge in those terrible days, our church. There, at any time, one was likely to find poor souls before the altar or in the pews seeking strength and courage as one after another of their kinfolk fell.

The darkest day was a Sunday. All day people had been going in and out of church and only morning and evening services were held, although the minister and organist had been at their posts all the time.

It was late afternoon when I entered and as I appeared the organ began the voluntary of the evening service, the music stealing through the thick grey walls, creeping past the stout grey pillars that had listened to an endless succession of voluntaries. Years ago, perhaps, fair ladies had come to ask protection for their knights who had ridden gallantly away to wrest the Holy Land from the hands of its captors.

Gently I tiptoed to a bench near the back of the church and knelt to pray. After a few minutes I stopped to listen to the comforting music. There were not many people in the church, just here and there a quiet figure kneeling with bent head. At the altar two black-clad women crouched held fast to each other's hands.

It was cloudy outside and consequently the church was dim but, surrounded thus, by friendly darkness and solaced by the soft chords of 'Abide With Me', I felt more at peace than I had for days.

The minister rose and going into the pulpit murmured a few words of prayer in his clear rich voice. As he finished a step was heard, and a hurried whisper. As I raised my head the church was suddenly transformed!

The sun had broken through the clouds and as the minister raised his arms above our heads and said in a broken voice, "My children, my children," a shaft of sunlight streamed across the pulpit and transformed his white hair into a halo which gleamed about his gentle face. Tears were streaming down his cheeks and, as startled heads were lifted he continued in a clearer voice, "My children, news has come; we have won a great victory!"

There was a dead silence, then heads went down again and a muffled broken sobbing of relief throbbed in my ears.

"Victory! Victory! Dear God, I thank Thee!"

Then I knelt to honour those who had fallen.

Barbara

I am the proud owner of a medal left to me by my grandmother. The medal has two bars, each bar signifying six months service for the Imperial Munitions Board during WWI.

There were very few Canadian factories producing shells when war was declared in 1914. Quickly the government established a Shell Committee and by May of 1915, munitions factories were established across Canada. In December the Imperial Munitions Board was organized and the hiring of females was encouraged.

Advertisements stated that girls under 18 need not apply although many did and gave a false birth year. Slogans urged women to do their bit for the war effort, and a popular song at the time was "Ammunition Girl". Reports on bad working conditions or poor treatment of the female workers were suppressed and by 1917, 30,000 women were employed in Canadian munitions plants.

At first, all supervisors were male. Resenting the entrance of women into their domain, their behaviour was less than exemplary. In small and large ways it was made clear to the women that their presence was not desired. A lack of cooperation, undeserved complaints to management, incorrect instructions to staff, verbal and physical abuse all played a part in the campaign to show women their place was at home, not in a munitions factory.

The women found ways to deal with the additional stress placed on them and became loyal, good workers. Eventually they were able to assume supervisory positions and employers recognized their value as production increased. Wearing khaki or blue coveralls and gloves to work the assembly line, the women were described as 'blue devils'.

Wages were low. A worker was fired if found carrying matches. Everyone was exposed to toxic materials. Accidents were frequent. Most workers feared lightening storms, when the buildings could shake and set off raw explosives.

A dangerous process was the feeding of cordite, which resembled brown sugar, into a press. The resulting spaghetti-like material was then batched by the workers, who called it rope.

The Scottish novel *Where the Wild Thyme Grows* describes similar conditions. Women workers were distrusted, men were resentful of their presence, and it took some time for acceptance by their male colleagues. These women also handled raw explosive materials. One of their duties was to tamp down explosives into empty shell casings to eliminate air spaces. Toluene made their skin turn yellow as it became stored in their fatty tissues and earned them the name 'canaries'.

The special gloves supplied for safety were clumsy and increased the danger of spills when casings became slippery. Some women disobeyed the rules and removed their gloves. Tiny fragments of phosphorous came in contact with their skin causing burns which quickly turned septic. Some of these sores turned cancerous and the women died.

My grandmother worked for at least a twelve-month period, and possibly more, in this challenging factory environment. We've often wondered if her health problems in middle age were, in part, a legacy arising from poor diet as a child in combination with long exposure to toxic munitions components.

A film on the subject confirmed my view of the work as hard and very dangerous. The film '*And We Knew How to Dance*' was produced decades after the war by the National Film Board, and sketched the experiences of women who volunteered their services as ambulance drivers, nursing sisters, farm hands, and munitions workers.

I was very impressed by the personal interviews with survivors, which illuminated the camaraderie they had developed with their co-workers and how it reinforced their determination to meet the challenge of these dangerous wartime tasks. They were heroines, all of them!

Edith

My dear old great Uncle,

We were all so glad to hear from you & especially to know that you are still living & as well as a man can expect advanced as you are. We all extend our heartfelt sympathy with you in your sad loss of a dear wife & also your grandson (who died for his country). There has been several killed that we know around here. We all feel thankful that the late awful war is over, & glad to have peace again, to be proclaimed about Easter 1919. Food has been rationed & prices controlled for the last 4 years. Bread is now 9 per 4 lb loaf and butter 2/4 per lb. Glad to say we have had plenty. Hope you have. I must tell you father can still enjoy his pipe of tobacco & mug of cider in the chimney corner. He wishes to be remembered to you & would like you to join in his company some of these long winter evenings. We are having daylight saving time here put all clocks forward 1 hour until Oct 1st.

Dear Uncle I expect you will be surprised to hear this farm is to be sold so if we do not buy it we shall be shifting. Northcott where Mabel lives is also to be sold. She wishes to be remembered to you. Pitt's where aunt Clara lives is sold. She sends her kind compliments to you. Uncle John still lives at Tadbeer is quite well with 3 children but sorry to say his wife is away in asylum she has been troublesome of late. Uncle Albert still lives at Doble 4 children all quite well. Aunt Ruth at Withywine 2 children girl 11 & boy 2. They seem to be getting on better now talking of taking another farm. Uncle Edwin lives at Waldrons which is also to be sold. They are all quite well. I expect you will think there is going to be a pretty good clear out at Ashbrittle of the Heards, Goddards & Coles. Sorry to tell you Uncle Tom is dead the account of which I enclose. I assure you it was an awful shock to all of us. He worried about the war in regard to his eldest son who was called upon to serve in the army &

worked over hard. Tom (my brother) did his training but did not go to France.

Dear Uncle we all thank you for your kindness for sending newspapers. We thought of you & enjoyed reading them. We often talk of the jolly times we spent when you were here. Do wish you could come over once more to see us & end your days here in dear old England but I suppose you have ties. Mother sends her best love to you & hopes to receive several more letters from you.

We have all had to work very hard since the war, being shorthanded left with only boy 16 on the farm so were all glad to have Tom home again & have a good man also to up the fences which have gone down very very bad as the farm is likely to be sold. Land is selling very dear some making £100 per acre & letting at £10 per acre for 4 months. Mother wishes to be remembered to your daughter & hopes she will continue correspondence when you are not able to write. Hope this will find you quite well. You must please take care of yourself. Hope you have a kind housekeeper to do for you. Now I must close with kind wishes from Edith & fond remembrances from all to dear Uncle Tom. Hope this will not be the last letter you will read from us. We should all like to see you once more.

Goodbye from your loving Niece.

Barbara

I have a very short story to tell you:

Our family moved to Pointe Claire in 1931, and when my brother Taun and I were small, mother asked us to do a job for her.

Since the job was to transport books, we grabbed his 'Speedster' wagon and started up the street.

Back and forth we trudged that day, lugging small wagonloads of books between the houses in our neighbourhood.

The collection became part of a lending library managed by our mothers throughout the War, and satisfied their desire for new reading material while they coped with wartime shortages of paper and books.

After the war the I.O.D.E. housed the books and for many years they operated a tiny lending library in Larocque Park.

We were regular visitors, since bliss for us meant an apple, a good book and a quiet corner to read.

It still is!

Ross

The *Dorothy Lucille*, owned by the Janes family, Ed and Fred his son, was a 47-foot Nova Scotia schooner, a fine sailing and even racing craft, well known on Lake St. Louis.

Both were fine skippers, from Newfoundland, which reminds me of that Newfie legend – "Us don't have to know how to swim, us can sail." That was the truth. I recall racing, one day on the lake, in Ed's *Terra Nova*, a then popular P.C.Y.C. class of 19 footers; a heavy squall hit the fleet and many turned over or dropped their sails, but *Terra Nova* drove on, with the crew up on the wind'ard rail – took water but not enough to wet our feet, and sailed on to win! That was in May, and the water must have been damn cold. The spray was, anyway. AJAX was popular that day.

After much planning and final preparations, the *Dorothy Lucille* sailed from Montreal, June 17th, 1938 for the Lower St. Lawrence, with Mingan on the North Shore, as our hoped-for destination. That was a memorable journey. I was elected the official keeper of the ship's log and I still have a copy of it. Our ship's company was as follows:

Captain	Fred Janes
1st Mate & Engineer	Bill Tellier
Purser	Tom Mounteer
Bosun & Deck-hand	Ross Robertson
Pilot of Lower Reaches	Les Scott
Able Bodied Seaman	Ken Dolbey
Cook & Cabin Boy	Richard Hicks

We divided into two watches – 4 hours on and 4 hours off; we often sailed right through the night, depending on the tides and weather. Richard proved to be no asset; he was sea-sick most of the time and couldn't cook anyway. But he did provide one item of interest, bringing aboard a homing pigeon! It was a smelly, useless passenger; finally, after a day or two en route, it was released to fly home, it was hoped. Circling overhead, it seemed to decide on a flight path, and took off into the west. Unhappily, it was never heard from again.

Ken Dolbey liked his tea, and made it at every watch change – so inevitably I took up the same habit, and found it very comforting and energizing, in the cold and wet of June on the river! We found a use for every item of clothing – even using towels as scarves. Fortunately we were armed with mostly warm 'duds', including 'long johns', mitts, toques, sweaters, heavy socks, etc. – and found we needed them all.

Our vessel was not new, and its weaknesses soon showed up. One dark night, it was 'all hands on deck' to take in the fisherman staysail. It was flying from the main topmast, and we had left it up too long, with such a strong following wind, which was getting heavier by the minute. To see the 'watch below' on deck in their long underwear only, having joined us to struggle with that obstinate sail, was something to remember! The lesson – topmast not strong enough to handle the 'fisherman', so it was not used again.

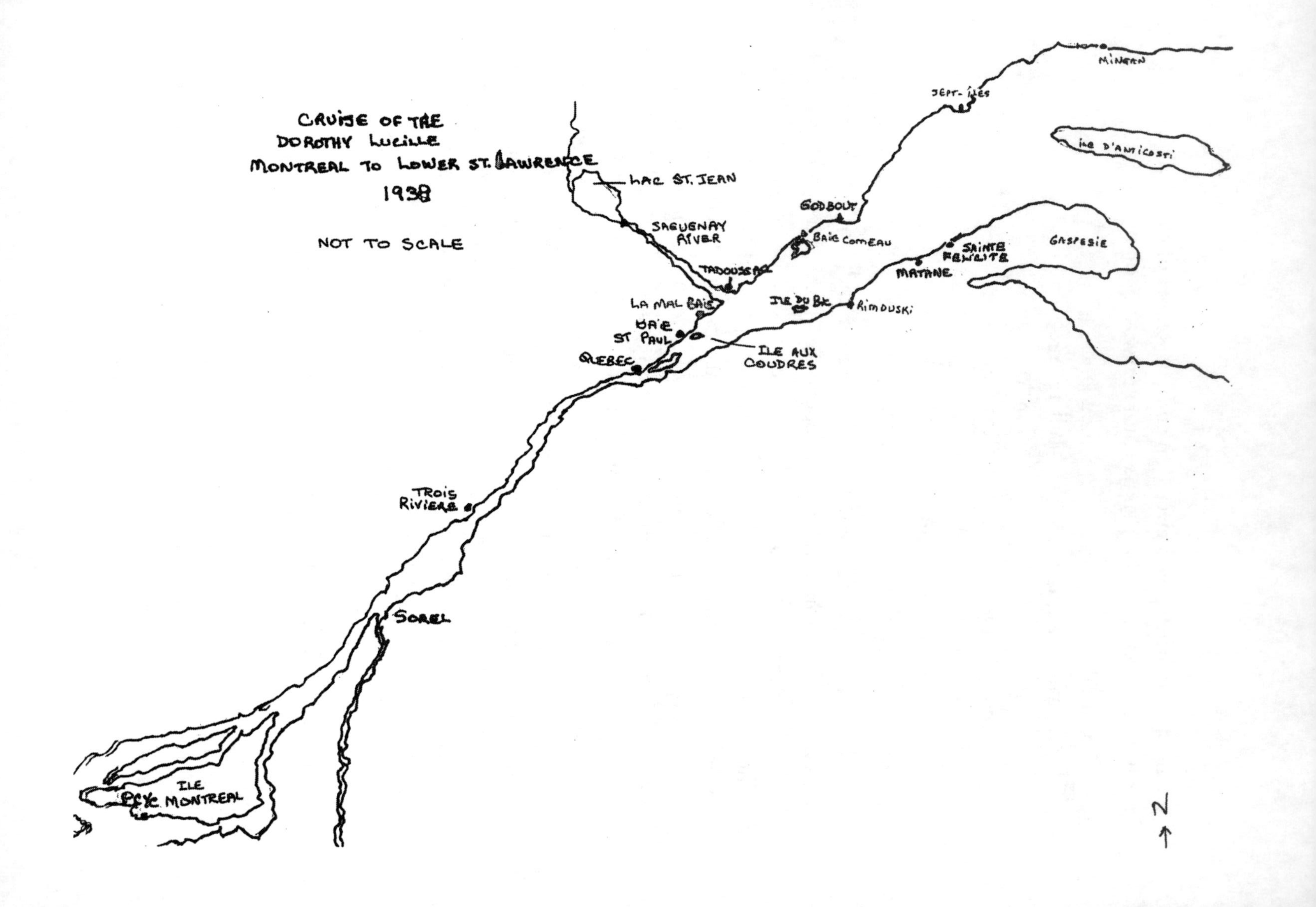
CRUISE OF THE
DOROTHY LUCILLE
MONTREAL TO LOWER ST. LAWRENCE
1938
NOT TO SCALE
LAC ST. JEAN
SAGUENAY RIVER
TADOUSSAC
MINGAN
SEPT-ÎLES
ILE D'ANTICOSTI
GODBOUT
BAIE COMEAU
GASPESIE
SAINTE
MATANE
RIMOUSKI
ILE DU BIC
LA MAL BAIE
BAIE ST PAUL
ILE AUX COUDRES
QUEBEC
TROIS RIVIERE
SOREL
ILE MONTREAL
N

Another problem was the dinghy – towed astern as was our custom in the sheltered waters at home – often full of water now from the breaking wave-crests. It would sail down the following seas, and seemed a constant threat to our transom. Eventually, we 'hove-to' in half a gale, and brought it alongside. Fred took on the risky job of bailing it out and attaching the halyards for hoisting it on deck. There it stayed for the rest of our cruise.

Heat in the cabin (and very welcome too) was from a small, coal-burning ship's stove; a 'knock-down' spilled it and live coals were scattered over the cabin floor! Fortunately the bilges were wet (as usual when sailing in the frequently brisk weather) but there followed a frightening few minutes, while all spare 'hands' tackled the emergency. Fire at sea is not a happy experience.

At anchor, off Bic Island, we had a day of rest, while the 'john' underwent major repairs. That was during our return journey, and I recall another fault which developed in the engine this time. We had left Bic, with the tide, heading across the river and upstream to the mouth of the Saguenay river; we 'blew a gasket' on the manifold and could only make temporary repairs, while en route and with only very modest tools and parts. Believe it or not, we wrapped it in some asbestos sheeting and bound that with copper wire! The mechanic who came aboard at Tadoussac shuddered when he saw our makeshift job!

We never reached Mingan – where Les Scott had lived as a boy, his father having been the Hudson's Bay Company 'factor' there. Les was a student of the stars, and many night hours, on watch, I was enthralled by his lesson in astronomy, as we gazed on that infinite display overhead! Not strangely, his business in life has been the fur trade, and the great outdoors his natural place, whether shooting ducks, hunting deer, trout fishing, or just striding through the winter forests, on snow shoes or skis, enjoying the silence and if need be just his own company. He was our Mingan 'Indian'.

Bill Tellier did not smoke but did have a powerful need for chocolate-covered marshmallow biscuits; our ship's stores contained an actual case of them! He always had a handy pocket-full as he kept his vigil on watch, in his favourite position on the fore-deck, leaning against the foremast. Bill's special job was 'engineer'. One night, with the mountainous North Shore on our lee, the motor sputtered out. I was on his watch and, in my unskilled desire to be helpful, wanted to know if I should let go the anchor! Bill commented that I would be a h--- of a long time hauling it back, if I lowered our long chain and anchor in that depth of water. "Keep your shirt on – I'll fix the damn thing." Which he did. Just a dirty carburetor.

Fred, as Captain, was also our sailing master and navigator. One run was 40 miles across the river, from Godbout to St. Felicite. A beautiful sail, on just one tack all the way, with a fresh westerly wind. About two miles from the south shore, I picked up the stone pier there (reading the chart), and we were right on! Not bad, with wind and tide, plus the varying currents in our great river. But we made most of our miles at night; it was easier to see and identify the light beacons, on that well-lit busy waterway than to do our point to point navigation in the daylight hours.

One example was while 'making our easting' down the South Shore, we ran aground! We later found that we were 2 miles off the point at Manicouagan (instead of 4 as we should have been) and were on that famous shoal – the graveyard of so many ships! We must have erred in our identification of other points of land during our run that afternoon. Anyway the sails were downed in a hurry. With, fortunately, a rising tide, and the quickly started engine, we managed to back off and bumped our way seaward. We carried on deck a rough-cut spar for use as a 'bumper', when tying up at wharves in those tidal waters. The whole crew laid on, using our bumper as a 'pole' to assist the motor, as we struggled mightily to clear those rock-infected shallows. We finally found and identified the doleful bell-buoy, which should have been on our port, had we been on the right course. Then, on a corrected compass course, as its lights showed up in the gathering darkness, we reached Baie Comeau.

Further east, a night or so later, we were in a dense fog, on a windless but restless sea, rolling miserably to the accompaniment of a grampus (a small whale indigenous to the lower St. Lawrence) blowing almost alongside. From our estimated position, the chart showed a small river (the Pentcote) flowing into the Gulf to the north of us. Under power, as dawn and a helpful morning breeze lifted the fog, we found the rock-bound mouth of the river we sought. A tiny harbour appeared and a sleepy wee village. Here was quiet, a hospitable people and room to stretch our legs.

Some of us went upstream fishing; others tried it near the river mouth (fewer mosquitoes). Heading inland, we found our way to the top of the hill behind the village. A forest ranger hurried after us to report distress signals from our vessel! Running back, sure enough, there she was, lying on her side in the rocky shallows, with the tide racing seaward! A forlorn sight. We borrowed a canoe as our tender was also in the mud on the other side. No harm had resulted although rocks were everywhere else; she lay on her port side, at a 45 degree angle however, until the tide returned, 12 hours later. Fishing off the river mouth, with our citified gear, brought no results except a 'crepeau', a sea-going frog-like creature which swelled up in an ugly way as it came to the surface. This was noticed with much loud amusement by the local fishermen, as they passed us, on their way out into the Gulf to catch their halibut. Their bait was salt herring, and they had freely shoveled over the rail of *Dorothy* what seemed like a bushel of them, for our evening meal. They are full of bones, but delicious! On their return, we watched them with block and tackle, lift on to the wharf two 200-pound halibut! They were promptly butchered and the housewives came down with pails and not a bit was wasted – the commercially valuable sections were set aside for sale to passing ships. While we hopelessly fished off the beach that morning, a small boy beside me with a rough pole cut in the woods and a piece of red cloth as bait, calmly pulled in some beautiful sea trout! I bought one for vingt-cinq sous and a broken trout fly from my fancy but useless assortment! He ran home full of glee; I was pleased with the trade, too.

Pentacote was a very poor village, deserted by a foreign pulp and paper company when the woods, after being thoroughly 'mined', had become unprofitable. Their employees had just been left to rot! In the winter they still cut pulpwood and brought it out by dog teams, to be shipped away on the decks of the coast-wise 'goelettes'; in the summer they fished. The inevitable priest was also Mayor, Notary, School-teacher and general factotum; their contact with the outside world seemed to be the nearby forest ranger and his radio. We saw no sign of any doctor. Their fierce dogs, chained in the summer time, were fed frugally on scraps of fish, and were thin and vicious. A little girl, acting as our guide in the village, calmly kicked them into quiet submission with HER BARE FEET, as we edged by! One evening we sought some milk, having heard that a villager kept a cow; everyone went to bed with the sun as any lighting was an economic problem. We found the house and a nightcap and tassle appeared at an upper window. She came out to us in night gown and bare feet to fill our jugs from a spigot on a wooden keg under the gallery; but first she had to wipe the spigot with a faultlessly clean AND IRONED linen serviette (it seemed to us). Their life style seemed a bit rough – one incident on that wharf was an altercation between a youth there and another below in a canoe – his brother it seemed – bad language was being exchanged and finally the boy beside us just picked up a 3 foot piece of pulp-wood and hurled it at his tormentor! Just laughter and jeers followed!

Everywhere we cruised, the hospitality was outstanding; whatever little they had they were glad to share with we voyageurs. We could do little for them in return. We did gladly accept a passenger, the helpful forest ranger, who needed a ride to Godbout, our next port of call. He was good company. The days rushed by. Rimouski, Matane, Mal Baie, Isle aux Coudres were among the fascinating stops.

We had little swimming as the river water was much too frigid for that pastime, but at one village we learned of a fresh water basin, in shore, and tried it out. Bathing trunks were not in our ship's stores but no matter. We reveled in that delightful bath tub and applied our little-used soap. Suddenly girlish giggles were heard and we glimpsed a row of gleeful faces peering at us over the rim of the pool. The village young ladies had followed us, guessing our destination.

Finally the smog of Montreal wafted over the waters and we made a memorable entrance to the harbour! The next morning, running before a strong easterly, we actually SAILED right up the St. Mary's current, past the Clock Tower, and into the basin at what was then called Black's Bridge! And somewhere I have a picture to prove it! Perhaps we were of that very few to accomplish that feat since (was it) Samuel de Champlain, headed as he thought for China, found and named LACHINE. Or maybe it was La Salle, another intrepid traveler. Anyway we figured we were pretty smart.

Our reverse gear had not been working properly, if at all, and maneuvering in narrow waters needed care. Entering the lock to the canal, we had to be ready with shore lines, to take the way off 'her'. I was ready on the foredeck with the bowline but found no attendant on shore to catch it! I rushed aft to use the stern line ready coiled there but tripped on a loose line left unwisely on the deck. I tumbled into the cockpit and went out like a light when my head encountered the binnacle!

Other than an ensuing quiet run to our home anchorage at Pointe Claire, so ended our cruise on the *Dorothy Lucille.*

Taun

The sun was bearing down without a breath of wind to compensate for the heat and humidity of the day. It was a typical Pointe Claire August afternoon in 1942. I was on my way down Brunet Avenue with a nickel clutched in my almost five-year-old hand to buy an orange ice cream cone from Mireault's in the village. The village was the commercial heart of old Pointe Claire, strung out along the Lakeshore Road, not far from the point of land which juts out into Lake St. Louis upon which sits the ancient old windmill of pioneering days. Sometimes referred to as 'le village', it is located about fifteen miles west of Montreal on the north side of the Lake.

Although the name on the front of Mireault's store was 'The Maple Ice Cream Parlour', according to an advertisement in the Lakeshore Press of August 5, 1938, the business was also known as 'Mireault Restaurant' with no apostrophe 's' after Mireault. In any case, whatever the official name was, everyone just called the place Mireault's, after the family which owned the premises.

Mireault's was a major focal point in our young lives. Located at the east end of the village in a commercial block near the corner of Victoria Avenue and Lakeshore Road it was easily accessible from our family home on Brunet Avenue, a block away.

The shop and restaurant started by Lucien Mireault was operated by his son, Roger. The business was open from early morning until late evening, so we had ample time to patronize the store. Roger seemed to be on duty all the time.

The advertisement referred above was to promote a new ice cream machine which had been installed one week before, a first of its kind in Pointe Claire. The Lakeshore Press also reported that 'large crowds' gathered to sample the ice cream, which was made from 'pasteurized cream, eggs and flavouring'. They could make 'any flavour' demanded by local clientele. My favourite flavour was definitely orange.

My route that day took me around the corner and west along the Lakeshore Road, which in those days was Route #2, the highway linking Montreal and Toronto. Mireault's was in a small commercial block next to the red brick pump house at the corner of Victoria Avenue. Across the Lakeshore road on the south side was another red brick building called the 'Poste de Pompier', a combined police and fire station with a tall tower of the east side topped with a powerful siren. The siren was used to call in volunteer firemen.

The entrance to Mireault's stood between two large glass display windows. In the summertime, they had one of those old wooden screen doors with a spring stretched across diagonally to keep it from warping. It always let in a few houseflies when it was opened and slammed shut noisily by itself when a patron stepped inside. Many of the flies were captured by sticky brownish-yellow flypaper hanging in coils from the ceiling.

There was no air conditioning inside but one or two large black fans rotated slowly to stir the humid air. In the wintertime, the fans were not necessary. Instead, for climate control, there was in the center of the brown linoleum floor near the ice cream counter, a large chrome grating providing warmth from a hot air furnace below.

Glass display counters ran down on either side of the store. The first half of the left case contained packaged confections such as chocolate bars and trays of bulk candy like gumdrops and jelly beans. The last half had the tobacco products. More smoking 'stuff' sat on top and on the wall shelving behind. The right hand display counter fronted the ice cream facility and was a sales counter for ice cream service. With a five cent piece, I was able to buy a single scoop of orange ice cream in a regular cone. There were no big waffle cones or sugar cones offered by today's milk bars. My scoop of orange always had little dividends of snowy white blobs of ice. This was no doubt due to the length of time which it took to make the ice cream. After mixing, a batch was frozen for eight hours before serving to customers.

Once, walking out the door, I noticed that my scoop had a dead housefly buried in one side of the ice cream. I merely flicked the carcass out with my right forefinger and carried on home.

One day when I came into the store with a nickel to buy a cone, no one was at the counter to serve me. What with pre-school age fidgeting, my coin dropped into the adjacent furnace grating and disappeared forever. Roger apparently saw what had happened from across the store. I was almost in tears from embarrassment. Roger very crossly asked what I wanted. Meekly, I said that I wanted an orange ice cream. He gave it to me, after which I quietly withdrew from the premises.

In the poorly lit rear of the store was the restaurant section which consisted of four rows of dark brown booths. A swinging door on the left separated the kitchen from the restaurant proper. I never ventured as far as the seating area. Orders from an authoritarian father were that no one in our family, especially my two older sisters, were to be seen there. The booths were a 'hangout' where smoking and other allegedly undesirable activities took place. The same directive applied to bowling alleys, pool rooms and even the local curling club.

At about age eight, I went to Mireault's with my brother and his buddy, Jim. The two older boys about age eleven were after chocolate bars. At this time in our lives, World War Two was still going on and wartime rationing was still in effect. For instance, the law called for only one chocolate bar per customer. I was too young to appreciate any of these regulations and the techniques used to get around them. When Roger came over to the counter, my brother asked if I would like to have a chocolate bar, too. Not having ten cents, I said "no." Wrong answer! I did not realize that he intended to pay for mine. Finally, I answered affirmatively. By then Roger frowned and furrowed his brow, knowing full well what the game was. He gave in and sold my brother two bars. We then left the store and headed home east along the Lakeshore Road. I really felt that there was a chocolate bar for me in the purchase and I looked up at my brother in anticipation for mine. Not a chance! My brother had no intention of sharing the two candy bars. Not even a bite!

Back in the Forties after the War and into the Fifties we continued to celebrate the birth of Queen Victoria on May 24, Victoria Day with bonfires and fireworks. It was an event to look forward to every year. Mireault's always had a large supply of all sorts of fireworks in the left front store window. For weeks prior to the 'Day', every extra nickel, dime and quarter necessitated a visit to Mireault's to augment the growing stockpile at home.

One of our favourite buys were rockets, each with a gunpowder fuel chamber and fuse plus a length of dowling out the back to give the missile some steerage. Even before Victoria Day, we used to go after dark to the grass boulevard down on the water at the foot of Brunet and fire them off towards the fleet of yachts moored in the harbour. Whether the rockets ever actually reached the boats, we could not really tell. Many of the daysailers had cockpit tarpaulins to keep out the rain and perhaps could have been ignited. Kids are not too good at anticipating consequences. Besides, the little rockets about two feet in length just looked so neat blasting off into the night with a trail of sparks!

Perhaps Mireault's has been described as somewhat run down but the store was typical of the day. The place was operated by a respectable Pointe Claire family which made a contribution to the community serving it with their store. Additionally, Mireault men were volunteer firemen. In 1937, Roger and his brother Maurice, who at that time were both volunteer firefighters for Chief Edouard Paiment, threw a party for their father, Lucien, who had been a volunteer for nine years.

Once, when I was still pretty close to the floor, I was in Mireault's one summer day buying something, when the siren on top of the fire station wailed an urgent call. Roger was behind the ice cream counter and immediately rushed around the end of the glass casing by the front door. Pausing only momentarily to remove the white floor-length apron that he always wore, he dashed out the door. I watched from the entrance as he ran to the fire station. The fire engine was already out of the garage starting to move east away from him. Roger kept running and leaped gallantly on to the back of the firetruck and away they went!

When we walked from our home to Mireault's, there was on the right hand side before reaching Victoria Avenue, a greenspace area which opened in 1936 in Laroque Park. It was renamed Memorial Park in 1943, with the intention of remembering fallen soldiers and accordingly to build a cenotaph after the War. The cenotaph was never constructed. This of course begs the question as to why not. Pointe Claire historian Brian Matthews reported that the list was lost!

Initially, the access to the park from the Lakeshore Road featured an overhead lattice-type archway at the center of the grassy and quite elegantly treed park space. At the center of the park, there was a green coloured hexagonal shaped bandstand where often-times a somewhat off-key local band could be heard performing of a summer's evening.

The Kinsmen Club held their summer fund raising tombolas on the flatter part of the park between the Lakes Road and the bandstand. When nineteen year old Doris Day had her hit record 'Sentimental Journey', one could easily hear the plaintiff song played over the carnival's loudspeakers at our house on Brunet Avenue.

By the time that I came of age to use the park, there was a two foot wide trail created by years of shoes and bicycle tires all the way from the corner of Victoria and Lakeshore diagonally across the grass up the hill to the top of the park at the west end of Julien Street.

If one walked up the path, the bandstand was on the left. Just beyond on the right there was a set of swings and a bank of seesaws installed in 1938. These play facilities were relocated from the lot where the new post office was built almost next door to the police station. Painted a utilitarian battleship grey, these playground items were constructed of thick wood with steel chains and metal support posts. They were built to last and even though children large and small tested the equipment vigorously, it seemed to survive.

Another foot trail ran to and from the Walford's white stucco house on Victoria and the once gated fence at the Julien Street entrance. The path was mainly a shortcut used by commuters bound for Montreal. These people went back and forth to the Canadian National or Canadian Pacific railway stations at the top of Cartier Avenue or Station Road as it was sometimes called.

When I started to use Memorial Park, the entry-way at Julien Street was only partially gated in that the gate itself hung only on one hinge. Both the gate and support posts stained green at one time were faded and dilapidated. As the years went by, the gate was removed finally or perhaps 'liberated' as a prank, never to be seen again.

There was another smaller flat area of slightly beaten down grass at the top of the path from the Lakeshore past the swings. There the trail sloped sharply upwards to the Julien entry-point adjacent to the flat section. If pedaling a bicycle, especially a standard bike without a gearshift, it took some heavy going to mount that slope. That top section of the park was where we just had enough room to play a bit of scrub baseball in summer, or simply 'horse around'.

My last memory of Memorial Park as it was then was when a group of us, both young men and women, strolled one evening across the top of the Park from Victoria to Julien. We had all grown up in the area. Perhaps some of us were thinking about our futures. However, I was too busy stoking the new pipe that I had bought from Roger at Mireault's the week before with some Edgeworth rum soaked tobacco. When I was finally able to get the thing lit, a lovely girl that I had know since grade two looked over and admonished me saying: "Taun, you are just trying to look older than you really are." Her statement was only partly true. That tobacco was an intoxicating brew and the aroma was delightful. Nevertheless that pipe quickly disappeared into my jacket pocket never to be used again!

Back around 1940, one store that our family frequented was a Dominion store at the corner of Cartier Avenue and Lakeshore Road in the same block as Mireault's. Dominion was a well known grocery chain and this store had the overhead striped awning over the front doorway which was typical of the period. My mother often shopped there because, like Mireault's, it was close to our Brunet Avenue home. If a larger order was required, she could use my brother's or my wagon to bring home the purchases. In winter, she had a sled with a substantial wooden box nailed on the top. It was easily hauled along the sidewalk with a loop of manila cord, the ends of which were attached to the front toe of each runner. Periodically, I picked up a grocery item there. One purchase that I yet remember was ten pounds of potatoes in a kraft bag at a cost of eleven cents.

It was at the Dominion store that I was to meet at age four, a fellow named Ted. My introduction was an abrupt push from behind at the front door as I looked down the concrete steps to the sidewalk. Suddenly I was at the bottom of the steps on the sidewalk looking up. Ted's mother apologized for her son's aggressiveness and I survived without physical damage. In the late Forties, when we moved up to Condover Road closer to Ted's house on Belton, we used to hang around together quite a lot.

By the mid-Fifties, Dominion had moved out of the above location. The site re-opened as Laplante's grocery store. This business was a full service grocery store which as such permitted the sale of beer. The store was staffed by Mr. Allard and Mr. Legault, both of whom my family knew from their years in the village grocery trade.

When we sailed or partied at the Yacht Club a block or so away, we would buy our beer from Laplante's. The procedure was to walk in and say hello to the two gentlemen who always seemed to be near the cash counter. We would then proceed to the cold storage room at the far right in the rear of the store where the meat and cold beer was located. There we would swing open the heavy insulated door, go in, and bring out a twelve-pack of pint bottles of whatever brand we liked at the time. Then we would plop the case on the counter, pay for it, say good-bye and head back to the Club. This went on frequently for years through my teens and early twenties until my business career took me to other parts of Canada.

Fifteen years later I was visiting Pointe Claire and was at the Yacht Club for a sail. Requiring a case of beer for the group, I went up to the corner store. It was still called Laplante's! When I entered the store, Mr. Allard and Mr. Legault were still there at the front counter! They actually recognized me as I waved and made my way to the cold storage room. After making my selection, I made my way back to the front counter and paid for the beer. It was as if I had never left Pointe Claire. I could not believe it!

Across the Lakeshore road from Laplante's sits the Pointe Claire Post Office. An imposing structure built of stone, it was put up in 1938. As a little boy, I quite often had to go in for stamps to take home. From the front door, there was a seemingly long very imposing hardwood floored chamber with windows on the left and a wall of post office boxes. At the far end of the room there was at the inside corner a black iron grilled wicket for the postmistress. My footsteps literally echoed as I gingerly made my way to place my order. There, looking upwards to the barely visible person behind the wicket, I would invariably be served by an officious, apparently unilingual francophone lady who appeared unfriendly towards little boys. My, how I dreaded those trips to the Post Office.

A few years ago, I accompanied my sister, a busy writer and researcher, to the Post Office to check the weights of her envelopes and send them on their way. The room with the wall of postal boxes seemed smaller than almost sixty years before. The dreaded unfriendly iron grilled wicked was no longer to be seen. It had been replaced by an open office area fronted by a counter. The new facility was staffed that day by two uniformed postal clerks. They were having a good old chit-chat at the back of the office. These fellows kept right on talking even although they obviously knew that customers were waiting for service. Finally one of them sauntered forward and asked what we wanted. Going out the door after our business completed, I asked my sister what was the matter with these people? Her response was that this was a typical attitude of some of the staff serving the public at this location.

More recently, I ran into a similar public relations posture near our summer home in the Laurentians. A new provincial liquor store opened in a community closer to us than the store we had been patronizing. The first day that I shopped at the new store, I tried to chat up the manager who was doing cash at the time. I commented that I had withheld buying liquor elsewhere so that I could support his new store. He shrugged his shoulders and said in these exact words: I don't care! !

In 2006, I had to drop into the Pointe Claire Post Office. There was only one person on duty at the time. He was a marvelous fellow, serving some housewives and myself in a friendly efficient manner, using his excellent command of French or English, whatever tongue was needed to get the job done. Sure wish someone like that had been around when I was growing up!

Proceeding west along the north side of the village, not far past where the Pointe Claire Theatre would be built after the War was a famous general store which had been established by Mr. R.A. Deparois in 1921. For a couple of years it was the only general store along the Lakeshore between Lachine and Ste Anne de Bellevue. Liquor was sold from the premises before the Quebec Liquor Commission built an outlet near the top of Cartier Avenue in the Fifties. What the store was called in 1921 is uncertain but by 1930 the business was named the Victoria Independent Store. However, like Mireault's the legal name did not matter. The general store was called Deparois after the name of the man who owned it. The only thing that I can remember about the store was the hardwood floor and strangely enough, mops and brooms. There is a reason for this memory lapse and a story behind it.

When I was a preschooler our family used to shop there. One day my mother was at the store to pick up some supplies. Instead of taking Canada Dry ginger ale to the cash area, she had selected two quarts of a less expensive brand. The man at the cash looked at what my mother had selected and said "Cheapskate, eh?" Well, she was mortified but walked home with her purchases and told my father what the man had said to her. My father went ballistic and immediately marched from our house on Brunet to Deparois' with the ginger ale. Dad said that by the look on the cashier's face the man knew that he was in big trouble. My father loudly 'chewed out' the poor fellow so that all of the customers in the store could hear about how my mother had been insulted. Looking back, I suspect that the man, with French as his first language, and trying to be friendly in a teasing manner, did not appreciate how unhappy an English speaking person would feel being referred to as a cheapskate. Nevertheless, no one in our family was ever again permitted to shop at the store! That incident is why I have such little recall as to what it was like inside Deparois' store.

Periodically, particularly if one owned a boat, it was necessary to visit Portelance's blacksmith shop which was situated on the north side of the village off a side street. This business had a long history of operation starting with carriages and evolving to customized truck fabrication. Before there was a marina facility at the Yacht Club, there was an anchorage in Pointe Claire harbour. All the moorings had to have a float, usually a metal drum, the larger the boat, the bigger the drum. One required the services of a blacksmith to encircle the drum with two metal straps welded into position. The strap was configured on each side and bolts put into place so that a shackle or two could be attached. One would secure the float to the weight on the floor of the harbour. The other side of the strapping would have a place for shackles to attach one or two mooring lines to the boat. On the bottom of the harbour, yachtsmen could employ a railcar wheel or perhaps just an enormous block of cement as an anchor weight. Although Mr. Portelance was busy he always looked after our boating needs with dispatch.

A door or so past Mrs. Still's gift-shop on the north side was Mr. Demer's butcher shop. It was a small store but always busy. They had sawdust all over the floor probably to soak up any 'goop' that might land on the floor. There was a display counter just inside the store on the left and behind the glass was a meat display, while on top was the one weigh scale. In addition to Mr. Demers, there were two, if not three other butchers to serve their customers. The men were always rushing to the cold storage room at the far end of the store behind the counter. The cacophony of various voices giving and taking orders on a busy day was always added to by the opening and closing with a loud clank of the freezer door. Mr. Demers himself was a short heavy set man with a somewhat ruddy complexion and a blond handlebar mustache. A classic persona!

My mother knew how to stretch mince meat a country mile. She had to with four children to feed. When it was time to prepare a meal of hamburgers or meat loaf, she did not need today's hamburger helper found on supermarket shelves. She used all sorts of her own additives such as bread crumbs, egg and onions to name a few. To start off with, it was not good to cook with just regular hamburger, because it was too high in fat which would disappear when cooked, and leave one with less meat than anticipated. The answer was to buy only minced sirloin. So when shopping at Demers, the routine was for my mother or sisters to ask for a nice piece of sirloin steak. When the butcher arrived back at the counter from the cold storage room and proudly displayed the beef cut, much to his chagrin he would be asked to mince it up. Grinding up the meat was annoying for them I am sure, because they had plenty of hamburger of much lesser quality in the display case which they would have preferred to sell.

Our hair was cut by Mr. Leroux, the proprietor of the Leroux Barber Shop, again on the north side of the Lakeshore past the center of the village. He had two barber's chairs but, seemed only to use the one nearest the picture window. Kitchen chairs lined the wall on the left coming in the door. Along the right wall was a long mirror with a counter below holding bottles of lotions and hair oils plus assorted hair cutting paraphernalia.

The barber chairs were not much different from what we might see today. Each chair had attached to it a strap for honing straight razors used for shaving. Waiting for my turn on the chairs against the wall, I was fascinated when Mr. Leroux brought up that strap and stropped his razor quickly back and forth.

Even at a very young age we were allowed to walk through the village by ourselves to get our haircut. There was no concern about predators back then. We would wait our turn amongst the adults or other kids waiting their turn. Mr. Leroux always knew who was next. He was a good barber, too. As an adult, I never had a better professional barber than Mr. Leroux.

A smaller man with glasses and a small mustache, he was gentle and patient with the children. Turning one's head when he was about to take a snip was frustrating for him but, he took it all in stride.

For children he had a box covered with a floral fabric as a booster seat on the chair. I could not wait for the day when I would be old enough to sit in that chair without the need for the booster seat. Then I would be a grown up! In the same vein, I wanted my sideburns and the nape of my neck lathered and shaved with that straight razor followed by some nice smelly shaving lotion! Of course, young people paid less than adults and so did not get the full treatment. More to the point, what barber in his right mind would want to approach a wiggling child with a straight razor!

There were other stores that we visited less often at the more westerly end of the village. For instance, every year since a youngster I went to Lussier's shoe store on the north side to buy a pair of Sisman's Scampers. Originally they were light brown leather casual with a durable sole of hard rubber. A laced shoe, they stayed on one's foot and wore like iron all through the summer and into the fall. Buying a pair meant that summer was on its way. They were purchased for any purpose including trips to see someone important in which case a few dabs of shoe polish would allow the footwear to pass inspection. Then one day the manufacturer decided to replace the hardy soles with a crepe sole glued onto the upper part of the shoe. The glue did not seem to be strong enough for young feet and the crepe sole would come off at the toe of the shoe. Fortunately by that time we kids were switching allegiance to a canvas and rubber running shoe, the kind that laced up over the ankles. They were neat to wear with jeans. So Mr. Lussier still looked after our needs.

Mr. St. Denis had a hardware store fairly close to the corner of Golf Avenue. He specialized in bicycles made by Canadian Cycle and Sports (CCM) and this is where I bought my first and only bicycle with money earned from the delivery of the Montreal Gazette in the Cedar Park area. The bike was a size 28 frame standard bicycle which would enable me in future to get through my route faster as long as there was no snow on the roads. It was my mode of transport until I bought my first automobile.

Across the Lakeshore Road from St. Denis' Hardware Store was an historical structure which housed the only drug store in the village: Dr. Martin's Rexall Drug Store. In 1920, the building was the Canada Hotel. It was and still is a longish storey and a half with a tin roof and dormers in that picturesque Quebec tradition, a design one can still see in rural parts of the Montreal region.

According to a Lakeshore Press article of June 7, 1940, Dr. Jean Baptiste Martin arrived in Pointe Claire in 1913. Too ill to practice medicine, he opened the store in 1916. We wonder if the drug store leased space from the Canada Hotel. By 1940 Dr. Martin had died. One assumes that Claude Letourneau took over the business soon thereafter.

With my bicycle, I was able to pick up prescriptions for my maternal grandmother Kathleen Scott who lived at the Daoust farm on the Old Lakeshore Road in Beaconsfield.

When my two older sisters reached puberty, our mother, supposedly in the interest of teaching independence, would not include their sanitary napkin needs with her discreet bulk order from Eaton's Department Store in Montreal. The girls had to bike down to Letourneau's Rexall on the family's only ladies bicycle with handlebar basket and twenty-five cents in hand whenever necessary to buy their own plain-wrapped package of napkins. Then they had to put their purchase in the see-through bicycle basket and self-consciously drive back home through the village. The girls felt that everyone who saw them, including any boyfriends who might be around, knew that they had their period. Growing up in a small town can have stressful moments.

Further east in the same block, if my memory serves me correctly, was the only five-and- dime store in the village. That was at least until a Rossy's opened up in the late Forties in the north side center of the village approximately where Deparois' store had been. The store that I refer to was run by Mr. and Mrs. Trottier and accordingly was called Trottier's.

One day I was in front of Trottier's ready to go in with my friend Brian, whose family had built a new home after the War on Julien Street close to our place. Brian had already entered the store when mounting the sidewalk some steps behind I saw a chap I had seen at Cedar Park School, our elementary school. Everyone called this boy Pinocchio for no doubt unkind reasons. I never knew his real name. Well, I walked over to him as he walked along the sidewalk in a westerly direction saying: "Hi

Pinocchio, how are things going?" When Wham! I received a mouthful of knuckles and an angry: "Don't you call me Pinocchio!" I rejoined Brian in the store who was no doubt curious about my fat lip. Still in a state of embarrassment, I was not prepared to discuss the matter.

In the next block to the east when I was a preschooler was Legace's bakery. This business was on the corner of a side street. Down behind the front of the bakery stretched a building which housed the ovens where the bread was made. Back in the early days of my life, bread and other products were delivered by horse and carriage in summer and sleigh in the winter.

Later on, the front of the building, when Legace's closed their operation, became a restaurant and the only bus stop in the village for the Provincial Transport Company. There one could buy tickets ahead of time for a trip to Montreal or Ste. Anne de Bellevue. The business was owned by the Boileau family. There was a son, Louis, who was the only person, boy or girl, who bested my older sister Diane in a scrap when they were kids. He belted her with his hockey equipment bag which had his skates in the bottom. When Louis grew up, he became the top boxer in the Air Cadets. The Boileau family had another son named Marc who became a hockey star in the American Hockey League. His poster size picture in a face-off stance was proudly displayed on the left hand side wall of the restaurant as one came into the store. One other member of the family was a boy about my age called Luc. We did not communicate when we saw each other. Perhaps we were each trying to decide who would win if we ever did battle. If he had been a hard-noser like his brother Louis he would probably have cleaned my clock!

Other than grocery stores, our favourite, most-patronized store was Cousineau's hardware store in the block next to the Banque Canadienne Nationale in the south side center of the village. They had in stock what seemed to be every dry good product on the market. Merchandise for sale even hung from the ceiling of the store. Great for Christmas shopping, which we often did, and every day hardware requirements.

Although I knew Mr. and Mrs. Cousineau to say hello to, I usually approached their son Vince, a tall thin young man with a high pitched voice who spoke English as well as French. He learned good salesmanship at an early age, trying to make me feel that I was an important customer by calling me Mr. Robertson even in my pre-teen years. He encouraged boating people to come to his store by keeping a special drawer near the sales counter full of galvanized sailboat hardware such as cleats, shackles and pulleys. As junior sailors at the Yacht Club, whenever we needed a fitting for our boats, we would go up to Cousineau's to check with Vince.

Vince publicized the Cousineau business by being supportive of baseball which thrived locally in those days. A photo in the Lakeshore News of May 13, 1948 shows Vince signing up players for the team that he sponsored for the 1948 season. In the early 1970's, my wife and I became good friends with neighbours across the street in Moncton. They were later transferred to Montreal and took up residence in Kirkland. One evening while chatting by telephone, they regaled us about this fantastic hardware store which they had found in Pointe Claire village. I said to them that they must have visited Cousineau's hardware store. They said yes, and proceeded to tell us about all the interesting products for sale that they had found there.

Back in the mid to late Forties, space age toys were not really on the horizon. We kids were into cowboy "stuff". Wooded areas near our homes had not been replaced with new houses, although they soon would be staked out and trees removed to this end. While they lasted, these outdoor areas provided ideal settings for cap-gun warfare amongst neighbourhood boys. One year I had enough money to go to Cousineau's and re-arm. It was not long before I came out of the store with a pair of double holstered pearl handled six-gun cap pistols. The belt and holsters had all those beads and leather thongs enough to rival anything that Roy Rogers slung on his two hips!

Caps were made by the Kilgour people. They came in a red box of five rolls of fifty caps each roll. The rolls were a coil of red tape with little blisters of gunpowder spaced to work effectively with the mechanisms of most cap guns. If we ran out of caps in the course of a playday, and could not get to Cousineau's or ran out of money to buy more caps, we would shout through the wooded areas, "Pow! Pow! Gotcha! You're dead!"

Cousineau's store is gone now, and sometimes one can see a slim grey-haired Vince strolling through the village.

The Pointe Claire Theatre was a key recreational facility for residents in the Pointe Claire area and beyond. While adults might be able to access movie theatres in Montreal or Ste. Anne de Bellevue, young people without convenient transportation could easily take in a movie in the village.

Construction of the 518 seat theatre began in early 1946 and was completed by the fall on a vacant lot on the north side of the Lakeshore Road at the eastern end of the village center. It was not that far from the Pointe Claire Hotel on the south side. Actually the project was undertaken by the owners of the Hotel. Brothers George, Lionel and Maurice Arpin shrewdly made the investment. Maurice Arpin lived around the corner from us on Drayton Road and was a familiar figure to us down on Brunet. He had been manager of the Banque Canadienne Nationale and would later become a popular mayor of Pointe Claire in 1956.

Investing in a movie theatre at that time was a good strategy because television had not yet arrived in our homes. Additively Pointe Claire began to move in the number of housing starts after the War.

Alternatives to a formal theatre for moviegoers were restricted by inconvenient travel restrictions. The drive to the Rex Theatre in Ste. Anne de Bellevue (Ste. Anne's) was seven miles along the Lakeshore Road. Bus service was possible. We were sometimes fortunate to go in a friend's car.

Before my time there had been a train service which took patrons from Pointe Claire to Ste. Anne's and back for a decent bedtime hour.

Vaguely, I recall a matinee to which my mother took us by PTC bus on a sunny day to see what was an appropriate family movie. When only four years old, I remember that my father's friend took the kids from our families in his automobile to see the cartoon, "Bambi" at the Rex Theatre.

The program that evening was a double bill. The second film was: "The Thin Man", which many will recall as a murder mystery, one of a series of movies where the famous amateur detective couple with their pet dog Asta, determine who committed the murder. I wanted to stay for that second movie so badly but it was not for preschoolers. So home we went.

One could bicycle up to Ste. Anne's as my sister did at age fifteen one evening with her friend Harry. After a long trek along the Lakeshore Road, when they tried to buy tickets to get into the Rex, they learned that Provincial regulations were being enforced which prevented anyone under the age of sixteen to enter a movie theatre without an adult.

The owner of the Rex Theatre realized that there was a ready market for a theatre in the Village of Pointe Claire back in May 1940, when he bought land on the north side of the Lakeshore opposite Dr. Ranger's office. This location sounds like the one bought by the Arpin brothers after the War. Rosenbloom's plan called for a four hundred seat theatre, a bit smaller than what the Arpins finally put up in that lot. The Rex Theatre entrepreneur gave up his plans during the War and put the lot up for sale.

As mentioned, Ste. Anne's was a possible movie going destination as was Montreal which had theatres on Ste. Catherine Street such as the Palace or the Princess. There was the Snowdon up on Decarie Boulevard, too. One might arrange to stay in Town after work, see a movie and come home on the midnight train to the Lakeshore. For young people especially, this was not a frequent scenario.

Until Pointe Claire Theatre opened, we saw movies regularly through the winter in the old gymnasium on the second floor south at Cedar Park School. A few days before Friday a flyer would appear on the notice board on the left hand side of the main door of the school as we went out. We would wax enthusiastic if a film featured our favourite actors. Of course, westerns were popular. We liked William Boyd as Hop-along Cassidy along with Gabby Hayes as his sidekick. Another likable actor was Johnny Mack Brown as The Lone Rider. Brown used to sing cowboy songs in his movies.

I should mention that these films were presented by the local Kinsmen Club. They offered a balanced fare in their presentations, and did feature films of more interest to adults. The kids attended anyway. The movies of more interest to grownups were for example: Bing Crosby and Barry Fitzgerald in "Going My Way" or Crosby again in "The Bells of St. Mary's".

As children, we lay out on the floor of the gymnasium in front of the seating area of folding chairs looking way up at the portable movie screen which was set up at the west end of the athletic facility. We were always restless and noisy and must have driven the adults to distraction.

The final alternative to see a film back in the Forties was home movies. My brother and I went to George Blandford's birthday party once when they lived near to us over on Bowling Green. On this occasion, I recall playing musical chairs, but not the movies!

However, once I was at the Wallace Siple residence on the western side of Pointe Claire village to attend a party to celebrate the birthday of his son Graham, who was a friend of mine from Cedar Park School. Mr. Siple showed movies taken by himself perhaps on one of his aviation business junkets, before he became an important figure in the World War Two Ferry Command which operated out of Dorval Airport at Montreal. The film that I remember included a beach scene in a southern climate wherein tall naked black men strolled about. "The Thin Man" movie years before would have been tame in comparison.

When Mr. Arpin opened his theatre, the seats were hard but the premises were new and well maintained. The films were current. French-speaking movies were shown on Tuesday night. From Wednesday through Saturday there was a double bill in English. Actually, it was more than a double bill because starting at seven the feature was followed by a lesser movie, then a repeat of the feature. Sunday and Monday there were new movies with a matinee on Sunday afternoon. Within the period of one week it was possible to see four movies and sometimes we did just that! It only cost us fifty cents to get in to the show and nothing extra to see a feature film twice. A complete show started at seven and ended at eleven or so.

A buddy and I stayed over one night to see once more Stewart Granger and Deborah Kerr in "King Solomon's Mines". All those years since, I thought it was an epic based on true adventure. Not so, according to an old copy of the famous book by H. Rider Haggard, first published in 1891. Haggard had spent considerable time adventuring in Africa, so his knowledge gave an authentic background to the novel, which was evident in the film. But it was not a true life story.

For the first four years of operation, it was rather warm inside the Theatre, until 1950, when the Arpins wisely installed very welcome air conditioning. They did not add a confection stand. We relied on a small store next to the theatre for an Eskimo pie or revel as we called them to eat in the movie.

Periodically, the Quebec Government authorities would force Mr. Arpin to adhere to the law disallowing those under sixteen to enter a movie house without an adult. Kids did all they could to look older. If one was tall enough and wore a more adult looking outfit he might pass muster. The tall, older twelve year old brother of my friend on Julien

Street would wear a long blue trench coat and gain entrance to our movie house. No matter what my age group did, we were doomed until the crisis passed and our entry to the theatre without an adult was permissible once again.

Kids sometimes dated and went to the pictures, or gathered there in a mixed group of both sexes. My first date was with an eye-catching redhead from Valois, a section of Pointe Claire a couple of miles east of Cedar Park where I lived. She was in my grade eight class at Cedar Park School. I could not stop looking at her and we ended up going to the movies in the village. As neither of our parents had a car, we had to use PTC bus service to facilitate getting together. She came by bus to the village wearing a nice dress and I met her wearing blazer and grey flannels. Nowadays, one would not even think of such formality just to go to the movies. The dressy clothes and public transport of yesterday makes today's movie date seem so much easier. And of course it is more relaxed.

When we as teenagers went to the Pointe Claire Theatre in groups of boys and girls, we usually sat at the back using up two or three rows. If we became unruly, Mr. Arpin's attendant would come with his flashlight and order us to stop talking. We surely made life miserable for adults who might have been taking a break from their own children.

One Friday night with our gang in a crowded theatre, when the air-conditioning did not seem to be doing its job, it was kind of hot in there. At an unfortunately quiet moment in the film sound, one of our gals simultaneously commented to the person beside her: "I'm so hot, feel me!" Well, because of the lull in the sound, the whisper became very audible! The audience roared in laughter. It was probably the best part of the whole evening's fare. Really tough on the girl who was understandably embarrassed.

Sometimes the Theatre was used as a meeting place for large groups which could not be accommodated elsewhere. For instance, fire prevention campaigns included an assembly of groups of students in our case from Cedar Park School. There was a bit of a stage in front of the screen to allow for speakers. Policemen who doubled as firemen would give a talk, ending with words from Chief Paiement. Now, Chief Paiement was one of the very best police/fire chiefs on Montreal Island, if not the whole Province of Quebec. Among many recognitions, he was elected in 1947 to be President of the Quebec Police and Fire Chiefs Association. However, we young people were irreverent as heck and afterwards summarized the concepts of fire prevention learned that day with the words: "If there's a fire, tell your father, your mother, your sister and brother, then run like hell!"

Pointe Claire Theatre had in the building a couple of shops on either side of the main entrance. The right hand side was occupied by the Lakeshore News office, a very good weekly run by the Freemans. The left side was leased by two ladies who ran a shop which seemed to be a cross between a drug store and a depanneur. When entering the store one was almost overwhelmed by soap and perfume fragrances which pervaded the store in a stuffy air which was hard to breathe sometimes. Whether or not they filled prescriptions or not was of no concern to us. Not only did they sell us revels mentioned previously, they supplied mellow rolls as well!

After a movie one could go in and buy a mellow roll in a double cone for ten cents. Vanilla, chocolate and strawberry were the flavours to choose from.

To prepare a double mellow roll cone, the server would have to peel off the cardboard overwrap of the ice cream roll and stick it into one mouth of the cone. A little push from the top of the roll with a piece of overwrap would secure it for the next stage of preparation. A single cone was relatively easy, but a double cone required some dexterity because the first ice cream roll was in the way. Of course, this all had to be done without the server touching the ice cream with fingers. No rubber gloves for food handlers back then. As youngsters, we watched every move of the server in anticipation of the treat to follow. Those mellow rolls were really smooth!

After the Arpins closed the theatre, the building was converted into a variety of shops. A few years ago there was a fashionable ladies clothing store in the front part of the old theatre building opening up on the Lakeshore Road. My wife and I with my sister dropped in to shop. The young saleslady when questioned was unaware that the store where she worked was once a part of the busy Pointe Claire Theatre.

Barbara

It was in June 1942 when my brother Taun and I first saw Montreal.

Ages five and twelve, we had been given permission to take the train from Pointe Claire to go into the city. Our instructions after we arrived in the city were to walk a few blocks north of Windsor station, then east on St. Catherine Street to our goal, Simpsons, where we could buy the very special present we were planning to give our Mother.

Excited after our first train ride, we emerged from the station and paused, intimidated by the huge buildings lining the streets. We were bewildered by the noise and the smell and the speed of the traffic, so different from our quiet village. We finally reached Simpsons, very hot and rumpled.

Smoothing our clothes and hair before tackling the revolving doors (we went around at least three times, I remember) we were then faced with dozens of enormous counters and aisles. Glancing at each other, we clasped hands for courage and went down the steps onto the main floor. We were determined to find the very special present – cotton gloves.

After many wrong turns, we found the counter displaying gloves and slowly chose our favourite pair, paying for them with money earned by delivering the *Lakeshore Press* at two cents a copy. We waited while the salesperson wrapped the gift carefully in tissue paper and put it in a box. Very happy with our treasure, we turned from the counter and began retracing our steps.

Back we went to Peel Street, down to Windsor station and through the concourse to the gate for the Lakeshore train. Later – much, much later, it seemed to us, we reached our stop and trudged down Cartier Avenue towards home.

Our big adventure to the city had taken most of the day. Dog-tired but content on this last part of the long journey, we looked forward to seeing Mum's pleasure when she opened our wonderful birthday gift. I cannot recall whether or not she liked the colour we had chosen, but I do remember that the gloves didn't fit her. We'd never thought to ask anyone about sizes.

Ross

One war-time summer Saturday, I was on the 8:15 A.M. CNR commuter train to Montreal – sitting as was my wont about midships in the car immediately following the engine. Such trains did not carry a baggage car there as they had little such business. Later, and as a direct result of the following occurrence, the railway commissioners required such a car to be there, if only as a buffer. We were to comment critically at the sight of the obvious union 'feather-bedding' – a baggageman taking his ease, as pipe in mouth, he enjoyed the trip in an armchair, in the open doorway, with not a thing to do. But on the day I speak of, he would have been an almost sure casualty!

As we rattled through the Turcotte yards (below the Montreal West escarpment), the coach gave a terrific lurch, and I sensed that disaster was imminent! I leaped down into the aisle and frantically clutched the lower metal seat frame! Glass, seat-backs, bags and people were flung through the air. The coach came to a stop on its side, and quickly was filling with smoke (we later realized this was mostly steam). The steam whistle on the engine had stuck in the open position and that ear-splitting noise, and the screaming of the people, injured or otherwise, were surely out of Hades itself!

The windows on the upper side were blocked – an engine, torn from its carriage, had settled there. I could see some light through the lower windows, and, kicking out the glass, managed to climb out through a 'water' filled ditch on to an adjacent track. What I thought was water later proved to be, in a large part, sulphuric acid from the broken storage batteries!

I stood there speechless (struck dumb in truth), and then was joined by two or three other escapees. We gave silent thanks, actually with arms around each other. Then something directed me back through that ditch and window into the coach. Maybe I could help some others. In there was chaos! Bodies were actually piled at the front end and, where they had been hurled by the impact, many badly injured. One was without clothes. Some 50 people were taken to hospital, mostly from our coach in fact. In the rear they seemed mostly to be standing, but trapped by the smashed door and vestibule – both ends of the coach had been 'telescoped' and normal exits were of no use.

Somehow, in the frightful noise and confusion, I managed to lead, pull or push some of those folk toward my escape route and out through the ditch. Even climbing over the broken seats and debris was extremely difficult – bear in mind that the coach was on its side. Workmen in the yard began to arrive to help, with ladders, axes, etc.

Dazed and injured people by the dozen, were sitting, standing or lying around. I noticed a freight office nearby and went there seeking water or something to refresh them. There was a soft-drink dispenser but the staff wanted money before they would let me take any to those poor people! I made a very angry speech (you better believe it) and picked up a hammer off a shelf and smashed the thing! Soon I had commandeered trays of ice and bottles and was busy ministering to my neighbours. My few cigarettes soon disappeared. I recall silent thanks for a lit cigarette from a man lying on a stretcher. Another was standing against a wall, obviously in pain from a badly crushed and mangled hand; I wrapped ice around it somehow and used his tie as a sling. Weeks afterward, a Bank of Commerce employee (next door to our office) came to the counter and identified himself as that man! His thanks for my little effort were almost embarrassing.

Things began to get better organized; a local train on the main line, following us, had been stopped and was used to transport other passengers and 'walking wounded' to the city. Our engine crew had been killed, also the engineer on the freight we had struck; his fireman only broke his leg, as he managed to jump free before the impact. Our own conductor was thrown and severely injured; he never worked again.

The cause of the wreck was found to be a switch which had been opened to allow the yard engine pulling a few freight cars, to cross the main line, to another part of the yard; the time schedule of the fast morning commuter trains had not been checked or improperly read – also we were traveling at too high a speed going through that busy yard, I would think, even if it was permitted, to make our carefully timed schedule.

Back to the story. That yard office had filled with passengers, seeking comfort in one another's company. I used their phone to call Dorothy and reassure her of my wellbeing, as the radio would likely be announcing the news of the wreck. I looked around the room and gave her the names of neighbours I could recognize, so that she could call their families and reassure them too.

Later, I found myself in the CNR (Bonaventure) Montreal station in a very bedraggled state, phoning my office that I would not be in. The Branch Manager, with little imagination, remonstrated at my plan to be absent – saying that they were very busy. I sought transportation back to Pointe Claire from the station master; he put me in the care of a crew member on the next outgoing local. I was 'secreted' in a wash room as I was a mess and no advertisement for the railway. He did feed me a cigarette but failed to inform me that his train did not stop at Pointe Claire!

I finally made it back home about 3 P.M. and as I walked in, Dorothy greeted me with tears; guess I was quite a sight. That had been a pretty exciting day!

Mary

The art of the story teller is something I really enjoy… the one who is able to frame the tales with experiences without smothering the stories being told… not that the personality of the teller is subjugated, but rather the teller is a facilitator and deals with the subject with respect and with joy in the sharing. The story teller is a special teacher… holding it in trust for the future.

Taun

Strangely enough, it was an automobile which launched my late parents into the world of boating.

As a young man, my father Ross had made a couple of canoe trips into the Lake Temagami area of Northern Ontario. He had also tried to join an eight-oared rowing team at the Toronto Canoe Club (Toronto Sailing and Canoe Club now). Dad's fingers were really too short to fully grip an oar handle. That first day, after Dad continued to catch crabs, the exasperated coach finally came over and roared across the water: 'You! Out!" Dad said he never went back to the club other than to sneak in to retrieve his rowing costume from the locker room.

Yachting however, was a different matter. He and my mother Dorothy became much involved with the pastime for over thirty years, sailing out of Pointe Claire Yacht Club (PCYC) west of Montreal. For Dad's part, he owned and sailed a variety of boats, did some club racing, served on race committees, took his stint as Club Commodore, cruised as much as possible and was the founding year President of the St. Lawrence Cruising Association.

Among many boating experiences was an epic two week family cruise in the summer of 1947. We cruised from PCYC on Lake St. Louis to Lake Champlain and back again aboard my father's first and only power boat.

The context of this tale reaches back to when my parents first came to Montreal from Toronto in 1929. After my father had spent some years as a traveling auditor with the Canada Life Assurance Company of Toronto, he had been appointed Branch Secretary in that company's principal Montreal office on St. James Street in the heart of Montreal's financial district.

With their infant daughter Diane (nicknamed Dinny), my folks moved at first to one apartment on Queen Mary Road in the Snowdon

Junction area. They sublet it and moved to another flat nearby on Earnscliffe Avenue also just off Decarie Boulevard. However, traveling beyond the confines of the city was difficult because Dad had parted with his first car, "Rose Marie", a four cylinder Buick Roadster, some years before.

One Friday evening after work, Dad happened to pass by an automobile showroom and impetuously walked in and bought a brand new six cylinder dark coloured 1929 Model A Ford Victoria sedan. He put down a cheque for one hundred dollars, signed a note for another eight hundred dollars and on Monday morning rushed to the bank to cover the cheque!

The new car made possible family excursions to the country, which included trips to the Lakeshore area of Montreal Island, specifically Pointe Claire, some fifteen miles west of Montreal on the north shore of Lake St. Louis.

The young Robertson family, which now included my sister Barbara, soon moved to Pointe Claire, a community which my parents would call home for the rest of their lives. In the thirties and forties, Pointe Claire was a quiet, mainly French-speaking shopping sector still referred to as "the village". It was surrounded by both permanent homes and summer cottages owned by a mixture of French-speaking and English-speaking people of wide economic backgrounds.

Pointe Claire and PCYC would become the focal point in the lives of my parents. They made many lifelong friends in this setting. Some PCYC members were from Pointe Claire vicinity. Many others commuted from Montreal or lived on their boats during the summer. The Yacht Club was sort of a poor man's club where members pitched in to run the Club and help each other enjoy the pastime of boating. If yacht club atmosphere had not been so remarkably spirited and if Dad had not purchased that new Ford sedan, probably this story would never have come to pass.

After my parents joined the Club in the early thirties, my father went into partnership with a fellow PCYC member George Mathewson in the acquisition of a grey, lapstraked sixteen foot Akroyd cat-rigged dinghy. Dad later bought out his friend's interest in the sailboat which was called *Bounty*. In a few years, Dad sold *Bounty* and ordered a new twenty-one foot sloop from Wesley Stevens, the famous boatbuilder located on Tancook Island at Mahone Bay, Nova Scotia.

To put the sloop on a freighter to Montreal, Mr. Stevens ballasted her with rocks from his beach and sailed her along the South Shore of the coast of Nova Scotia to Halifax. He told my father that he entered Halifax harbour while the Royal Nova Scotia Yacht Squadron was running a race. *Curlew* as Dad would christen her, apparently sailed very smartly through the fleet. Dad wrote that the boat was off-loaded from the freighter on a dark night down on the Lachine Canal.

Later at PCYC they had to put a metal shoe on the keel to replace the rocks that Mr. Stevens had employed, thereby improving the boat's righting moment. Dad built a cuddy at the forward end of the cockpit and modified the sails. They accomplished the latter by removing the sea-going bolt-rope from the leech of the mainsail and sewing in batten pockets. A boom was added to the loose-footed jib to facilitate tacking. My father recorded that he won a few trophies with her but one problem was never corrected, and that was the slight S-curve in the homegrown mast. She always sailed better on starboard tack! A sister-ship was built for Art Walter, Sr. whose son of the same name would marry my sister Diane in 1950.

My brother Ian was born in 1934 and shortly after I was born in 1937, the Ford Victoria was sold. In the early forties *Curlew* was let go as the cost of bringing up four children used up my father's limited resources. It was not until the end of World War Two, in the spring of 1946, that my father heard through the grapevine that there was a power boat available at the Royal St. Lawrence Yacht Club down the Lake at Dorval. At this point in his life, my father wanted a boat of any kind, sail or power, just so that he could be afloat again at the helm of his own vessel.

That same day, accompanied by Ian, Dad took the Provincial Transport Company bus along the Lakeshore Road to inspect the boat, which was sitting hauled out in a cradle on the maritime railway in the Yacht Club boat yard. They saw the cruiser as they entered the Club yard. The vessel was a thirty-foot round-chined Richardson class trunk cabin cruiser which had a shelter top with a vertical windscreen over the cockpit.

However, the boat was in a disastrous condition; a grey-painted hulk with any vestige of luxury stripped away or broken. Large black identification numbers "H.C. 98" displayed themselves on either side of the bows attesting to the boat's war time history as a harbourcraft for the Royal Canadian Navy at Sydney, Nova Scotia. She had apparently been sunk more than once during her tour of duty and the boat's condition really reflected its misuse. The starboard bow was bashed in, no doubt due to collision with a larger vessel or dock. The hull required repair below the waterline before it would ever float again, due to open seams between the planks.

Climbing aboard, a lifting of the hatch in the cockpit revealed what was once a six cylinder Grey Marine seventy-one horse power engine. The motor was now a chunk of rusted iron, having been attacked mightily by salt water. Down below, as outside, everything was painted grey including any dirt that may have been in the way of a seaman's paint brush. There were heavy wooden upper and lower berths on either side in the main cabin. Up in the forecastle was a marine head with a smashed toilet bowl. That is all there was in the boat! In any case, Dad's boating friends thought that the wreck could be fixed up, if he did not have to pay too much for it.

It was subsequently learned that the boat was owned by a Royal Canadian Navy officer based in Ottawa. He had turned over his pleasurecraft to the Navy when the war started. Dad telephoned the man from the office on Monday morning. He made an offer which resulted in a long suspenseful silence at the other end of the line. The officer then commented that he thought that he would get more for it but he accepted the offer. Dad was very close-mouthed about what he paid for the derelict and would only admit that he bought it for a song.

As the boat was, it was worthless as a yacht without an immense amount of creative work. Dad was an excellent carpenter but by no means had the tools nor the skills for fine finishing work or the rebuilding of engines. And that is where those great yacht club friends of my parents came into the picture.

Naturally, officials at the Royal St. Lawrence Yacht Club were anxious to see the unsightly wreck gone from their yard. So after a few weekends spent to render the boat seaworthy, she was relaunched down the marine railway and towed five miles upstream to PCYC. The 'tug' was *Margo V*, a pristine thirty-six foot Chris Craft sedan powered by two six cylinder Chrysler marine engines and skippered by Hugh McIntosh. Since the war, Hugh and Iris McIntosh had become close friends of my parents through the PCYC. Hugh was an electrical engineer with Bell Telephone and had spent the war as an officer in the Royal Canadian Navy. He was your compleat yachtsman and there was little he did not know about power boating.

The Richardson was hauled out and placed in the north yard of the club out of the way, while for the next twelve months an extensive overhaul of engine and hull took place. The engine was removed and taken to the basement of our rented home near PCYC to be worked on over the winter.

Unfortunately, that same winter Dad caught pneumonia and was confined to bed for about three weeks. While Dad fumed upstairs, four of his friends, over a period of weeks, had mounted the engine on timbers on the basement floor. They stripped it down completely and rebuilt it. Key people involved were of course Hugh McIntosh as well as Eric

Jones, Don Thomson and Dick Smith. Eric Jones was an amateur marine architect who had designed and built several sailboats. Don Thomson was a former pilot and owner of a forty foot twin engine Wheeler express cruiser named *Oracle*. Dick Smith was a former Royal Canadian navy officer. While his civilian occupation was banking, he knew power boats and was a fine cabinet maker. He became the key factor in the success of the interior reconstruction of Dad's cruiser. All of these men were familiar with marine engines.

One evening, as Dad told us later, he was startled by "an unholy burst of noise" which shook the house and "lifted me from my sickbed." The four men in the basement, having attached a battery to the motor, had actually started the engine! It of course made eminent good sense to be sure that the engine worked before lowering it back into the hold.

When spring came the engine was successfully loaded onto a truck and lowered once again into the engine compartment. The engine control panel box on the port side had to be redesigned with the proper gauges, throttle, and a new starter button. The original gear shift on the cockpit floor was still operational.

The brass three-bladed engine propeller had to be overhauled to straighten it and remove dints. There was a machine shop that reconditioned propellers in Cornwall, Ontario, about an hour's drive west of Pointe Claire. To get it there, one night Dad and I walked with it up Cartier Avenue to the Canadian National Railway Station. There my father made arrangements with the freight agent inside and tagged it with destination information. Then we went outside and Dad tossed the propeller onto the floor of a waiting boxcar and off it went to Cornwall. I imagine it came back the same way. It was a very unpolished but workable system of moving cargo around and did not require computers or high speed eighteen wheelers.

The first job in preparing the hull itself for reconditioning was to remove all the grey paint which had been slapped on everywhere both inside and outside by naval personnel. To repair the hull, the key ingredient other than elbow grease was white lead powder. Mixed with glazing putty it created an ideal seam filler after caulking in between the planks with caulking cotton. Mixed with varnish, white lead powder turned into a compound excellent for filling the many gouges in the planks, because it dried very hard and was easy to sand smooth. When Dick Smith rebuilt the bridge deck, he covered it with waterproofing canvas and glazed it with white lead powder and varnish to make it hard and smooth.

Down below, the heavy wooden upper berths were replaced with light pipe berths, which when not used as a seat backing were raised and hooked into carline in the cabin deckhead with customized steel rods. A relatively small change but the utility of the system was marvelous when cruising with a family.

Dick Smith built a new galley which he fabricated at home in his shop. He installed a large top loading ice box on the port side of the companionway. On the starboard side he built a counter for a fixed two-burner Primus stove and a sink with cold water from a water tank in the forecastle on the starboard side. A hot water tap hooked in cleverly with the cooling water system of the engine which in a thirty-foot boat was close by.

An invaluable cruising asset were the khaki canvas cockpit curtains which my mother and Dick Smith manufactured. When not in use, the panels rolled up conveniently under the inside edge of the shelter top. On rainy days, even underway, one could roll them down, join the panel zippers and snap the bottoms onto the outside of the cockpit combing. This created a large protected living area.

My Father christened the cruiser *Thalia Ann*. Thalia was the first name of one of his two sisters and Ann was the second name of his other sister. The name was painted on the transom in black letters and they showed up handily on the white paint of the transom. White paint was used on the stern of the boat because the original mahogany transom was too far gone from exposure and other damage to look shipshape. So early in the summer of 1947, *Thalia Ann* was launched and commissioned for a season of enjoyment and adventure.

There is no record as to when the idea of a cruise on Lake Champlain took shape but it was to quite an undertaking for Dad's cruiser to be taken on a trip so early in its refitted career, particularly when most of Dad's boating experience had been in handling sailboats, not power boats.

Father's main experience in boating waters larger than Lake St. Louis had been as crew aboard the *Dorothy Lucille*, a fair-sized schooner from PCYC. He and a handful of other men cruised down to the Lower St. Lawrence in the summer of 1938 for two weeks. This time however, Dad would be skipper of an untried refurbished power boat with a cranky engine. He would also be responsible for his wife and four children.

In trials on Lake St. Louis, *Thalia Ann* could achieve a maximum seven knots of speed but only for a short duration until the engine started to heat up. Then motor oil had to be put in the engine while underway and/or the engine RPM had to be cut back. One question in our minds was: with minimum forward speed long term, could our cruiser make it up the current of the Richelieu River at a satisfactory pace? What about the tendency of the boat to veer unexpectedly at times? This factor could be tricky in the narrow confines of the Richelieu. Upon our return to PCYC, would we be able to get back up the very strong rapids of the St. Mary's current at Montreal? What could happen with inclement weather and/or heavy seas that one could expect on a large body of water like Lake Champlain?

Whatever adventures there were ahead of us, and there would be many, we left accompanied by *Margo V* from PCYC harbour midmorning Saturday July 26, 1947. The third yacht of our little flotilla, *Oracle*, with Don Thomson and family, was delayed by mechanical difficulties but indicated they would catch up with us.

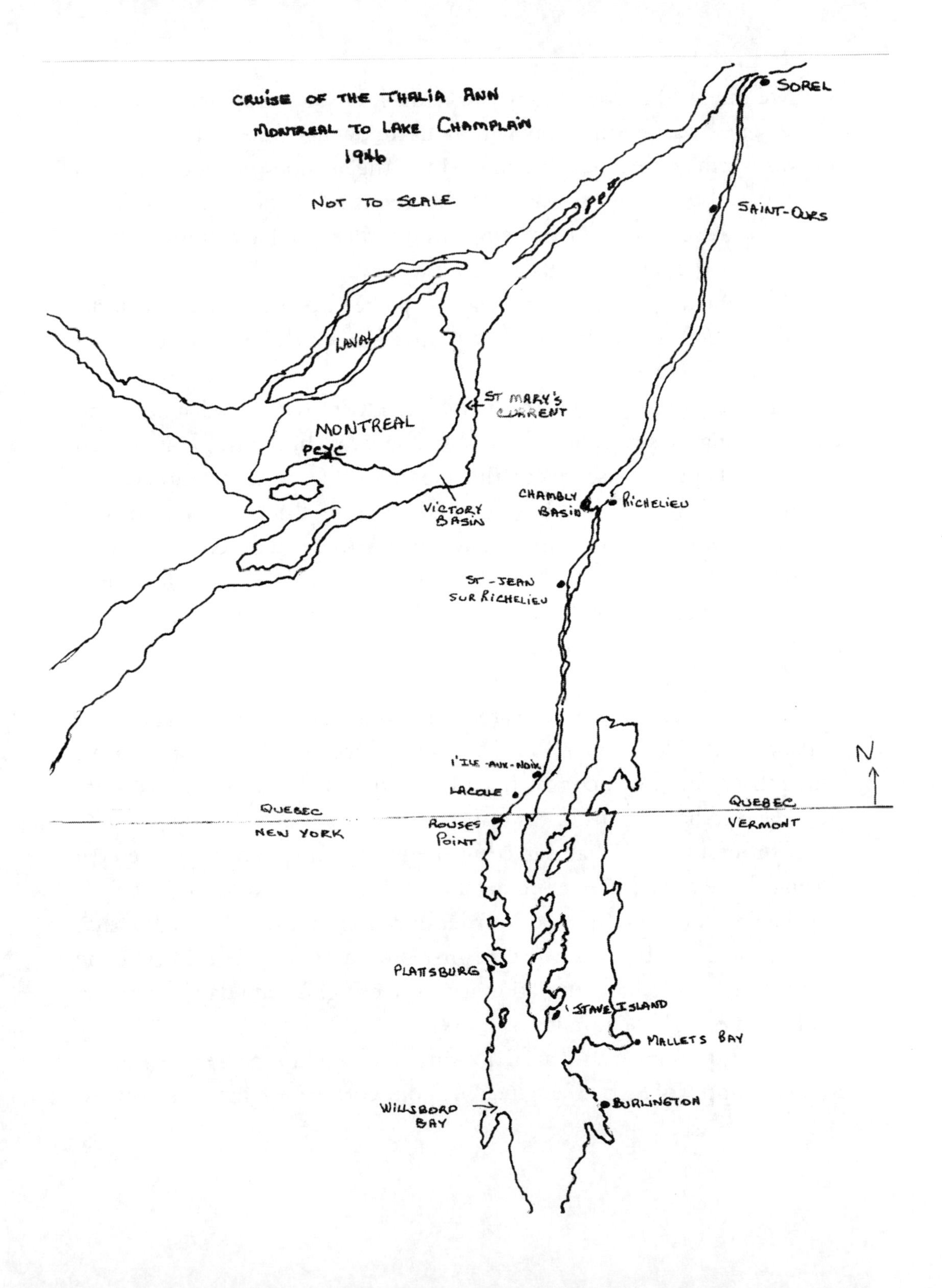

CRUISE OF THE THALIA ANN
MONTREAL TO LAKE CHAMPLAIN
1946
NOT TO SCALE
SOREL
SAINT-OURS
LAVAL
ST MARY'S CURRENT
MONTREAL
PBYC
VICTORY BASIN
CHAMBLY BASIN
RICHELIEU
ST-JEAN SUR RICHELIEU
I'LE-AUX-NOIX
LACOLE
QUEBEC
NEW YORK
ROUSES POINT
N
QUEBEC
VERMONT
PLATTSBURG
STAVE ISLAND
MALLETS BAY
WILLSBORO BAY
BURLINGTON

We followed *Margo V* down Lake St. Louise to the Lachine Canal. The day was warm and sunny with light following westerly breezes. The air was warm in the cockpit and cabin as the air does not more around much on a boat when forward speed is about the same as the following wind. However, that did not stop my mother from installing privacy curtains for the cabin portals while underway.

After locking through the canal, we picked up family friend Charlie Buisson at Victoria Basin and then plunged down the six knot rapids of the St. Mary's current.

Charlie was a retired Canadian Army officer with a tall stature and commanding presence, and a marvelous sense of humour. He had been in charge of enemy prisoners destined for Canadian concentration camps during the War. He would be of much help to my Mother the next day.

So, off we went down the St. Lawrence, arriving at Sorel around supper time, where we berthed for the night. The mouth of the Richelieu was just a little further downstream, where we would "turn right" and proceed south to Lake Champlain.

The little basin was rather full at that hour. *Margo V* found a spot, while we ventured further forward to find ourselves welcomed along the outside of the *Moosemin*, a Royal Canadian Mounted Police patrol boat. This pusser vessel was commanded by Corporal Ray Cassidy. We were privileged to have a tour of his ship.

Corporal Cassidy had served in the Royal Canadian Naval Reserve during the War and he well remembered *Thalia Ann* from duty at Sydney, Nova Scotia, and quoted the identification numbers 'H.C. 98' that had adorned the bows when Dad first saw the boat. He said that the "darn thing" had a bad reputation for its steering. After a day in passage, Dad said he could believe it.

One important errand after docking was to go up to a service station to buy a supply of SAE 40 engine oil, as our cruiser's engine had required one quart every two hours while underway! The cost per quart was 47 cents.

That evening we watched the beautiful Canada Steamship Lines passenger ship *Tadoussac* tie up at a reserved pier in another part of the harbour. Built in 1928, she plied St. Lawrence River ports entertaining guests with dining and dancing until retired in 1965.

We spent a comfortable night, except that the boat rolled all night. This was because we were positioned right opposite the mouth of the harbour where swells reached us from the wash of ships passing on their way up and down the St. Lawrence River. There was no way to stop our round chined vessel from rolling periodically but no other spots were available in the small basin.

The next day, as morning sunshine flooded the cockpit, breakfast was being prepared in the galley on the two burner Primus stove. On one burner there was a galvanized bucket of harbour water boiling and ready for the washing of dirty dishes when the morning meal was completed. Just as I was exiting from the head at the forward end of the cabin, another swell rolled our cruiser dramatically.

Moving aft, I saw Mom and Dad scrambling in the galley by the stove. The bucket of bubbling water tipped of the burner! Mom tried to grab the metal handle so that the water would not spill onto my father's bare legs. Instead, she plunged her right hand into the boiling water and scalded her hand!

The *Moosemin* had already pulled out at 0700 hrs. so no first aid was available from its crew. Word was sent for Hugh McIntosh, who with first aid kit in hand rushed along the dock and down to our cockpit. He applied some available olive oil liberally over my Mother's blistering fingers and thumb. Dr. Lafleur, a nearby Sorel physician came promptly to attend to my mother. He said that the olive oil had done an excellent job. Some sixty years later, we know that oil treatment of a burn tends to hold in the heat, possibly furthering damage. Would today's technique of just applying cold water have been a better route to take? Who knows for sure.

Irrespective of my mother's painful injury, our two pleasure craft set out to go up the Richelieu River for our second night at Chambly. We passed the Simard shipbuilding works where could be seen a fleet of some of the famous World War Two corvettes rusting away and a submarine called the *Seawolf* sitting there along with a one-half dozen landing craft.

We proceeded up river and arrived at the St. Ours lock and dam at 1330 hours. Ahead of us were nine locks with a total lift of seventy-four feet which would take us to Chambly Basin by 1900 hrs. Mother was still in terrible pain. From Sorel to St. Ours she sat on the settee at the after end of the cockpit while Charlie Buisson held her arm by the wrist and squeezed hard as the pain waxed. When she would burst into tears, Charlie would talk gently to her to help relieve her discomfort. Today I wonder why Dr. Lafleur did not give her something for pain. I suspect that there was not much available other than aspirin, which in Mother's case really would not have helped.

The run to Chambly was accompanied by a strong westerly wind across our beam. Combined with the strong river current on our bow, steering was troublesome and forward speed was slow. However, the channel was well buoyed and use of the chart was not required. We made fast to the east side of the pier near the Chambly lock entrance where there was plenty of water beneath our respective keels. The only stop we made was at St. Ours where Mom was transferred over to *Margo V* where on the larger vessel she would be made more comfortable.

The only persons at the helm that day were my father and brother. My two older sisters were never invited to take the helm, even although they would have relished the opportunity. Perhaps typical of the day, males seemed to have come first in my family.

Friends of my parents, George and Audrey Kyle came aboard for a visit from their summer home near Richelieu, Quebec. Mr. Kyle was an underwriter for Canada Life at my Father's office. They stayed for dinner on board, during which time plans were made to spend time together the next day. We took on highly chlorinated water from the top of the pier at the lock and picked up some bread nearby. On their way home the Kyles kindly arranged to send ice back by taxi. They had also brought word by telephone that the *Oracle* had left the Lachine locks at about 1800 hours on Saturday July 26 and that Don Thomson expected to join us at Chambly late Sunday afternoon July 27th. Everyone retired early with rain in the air. Surely enough it rained and stormed in the night but we were very comfortable.

Sunday July 27th we awoke to a beautiful morning and spent the first half of the day swimming. At noon the whole crew went to have lunch with the Kyles at Richelieu. Then the Kyles came back a second time for a short run in the *Thalia Ann*. A thunder storm turned us back to the dock accompanied by a heavy rain squall. We picked up two boys who were fishing in a boat and brought them back into shore. The rain was intermittent all evening but that did not put a stop to socializing.

George Kyle and Montreal acquaintances Dr. Brule and Major Thibodeau and his two teen-age daughters came aboard that evening. My two sisters went off to the movies with Mr. Thibodeau's daughters. They came back about midnight at which time all our guests departed for the night. Mom and Dad went over to *Margo V* for a night-cap and returned for bed at one AM. Mom and Dad never learned that the moviegoers sang ribald songs loudly all the way back to the boat. Our strict parents would not have been amused!

Nomad, a thirty-six-foot Chris-Craft cruiser from Iroquois Yacht Club at Lachine and owned by M. Dufour stopped for the night on the way to Lake Champlain. We would all by heading south on the next leg of our trip to Lake Champlain the next day.

On Monday July 28th we awoke to find the weather still cloudy with an occasional shower. Although the radio on *Margo V* promised clearing skies later in the day, the barometer that George Kyle had lent Dad was still registering low. Nevertheless, we locked through at noon and obtained more ice and water at Chambly. At the same time Diane, a nurse in training, as instructed by the doctor in Sorel, rebandaged Mother's scalded hand. Dad took the opportunity while at the lock to telephone St. Ours for news of *Oracle* and left a message there as to where we were on the Richelieu.

It should be noted at this point that whereas it takes about two days to arrive at Chambly by boat from Montreal, the way by automobile takes only one-half an hour. The community of Richelieu where the Kyle family spent their summers lies directly across from Chambly on the east side of the Richelieu River. With today's highways, it is only a short jaunt to go all the way to Lake Champlain from Montreal. Today, many boating people who live and work in Montreal find that buying a boat south of the border and keeping it berthed at a marina in the American portion of Lake Champlain makes good economic sense and provides excellent boating.

From Chambly, there were eight small locks and numerous bridges, which in spite of the high water levels at that time, were passed under without mishap. A late luncheon was eaten at 1500 hours. My father's log states that Ian was at the wheel as usual and was doing a fine job. The two cruisers arrived at St. Jean sur Richelieu at 1630 hours and found a handy service station right on the canal just upstream from the last lock into St. Jean. We took aboard 32 gallons of gasoline at 36 cents a gallon and *eight!* quarts of Mobile Oil at 48 cents each.

We passed through customs at Lussier to make a stop at Lacolle unnecessary and then moved on to the St. Johns Yacht Club where we registered and then relaxed for a swim in the river followed by refreshments.

Our only problem this day was the reverse gear, which seemed only to function ten percent of the time.

We met Pat Gerard and her mother Simone on the dock so they came aboard for a visit. There was a beautiful moon and the only distraction from the tranquility of the evening was very noisy swimmers at the government wharf nearby. We decided to have our own late evening swim before retiring.

On Tuesday, July 29, we arose at 0730 hours where the first order of work was to tighten up the reverse gear and repair the pilot seal on the stuffing box, which had come adrift during Monday's leg of the cruise. The propeller shaft passes through the pilot seal and the stuffing box on its way to the propeller outside the hull. Leakage can occur here and Dad must have checked this while improving the reverse gear function.

We caught up with *Margo V* around 100 hours at Ile aux Noix, which was a popular anchorage. *Thione*, a forty-foot yawl owned by Judge Charbonneau of PCYC was moored upstream of the island. So the three yachts rafted together for lunch. On board *Thione* was the Judge's attractive daughter, Mireille (Mimi), a little older than my sisters. She had had the opportunity to become an excellent sailor handling her father's boat while growing up. I believe that she did not have brothers!

Our two boats reached Rouses Point by 1715 hrs. at the United States-Canada border and anchored in the bay above the swing bridge opposite a marine products facility. American Customs and Immigration officers arrived by water, came aboard and were very pleased during their inspection. However, not so the official at Lacolle back downstream, who called us back in because we had not cleared customs using his office. My father wrote in his log that it was a "lot of nonsense but who cares!"

While we were back at Lacolle, a young chap committed suicide in front of everyone by diving into the river off the pier. He just never surfaced again. Apparently he had said goodbye to his family before ending his life. We may think youthful suicides are a problem of only today's young people but they took place sixty years ago, too.

On Wednesday, July 30th, we were anchored behind the Rouses Point breakwater. When the boats were safely squared away for the evening, the adults partied as much as possible. It was not too long before Rouses Point was renamed Souses Rout.

In spite of the weather we had seen building up in the southwest at 1900 hrs. we spent a quiet night at anchor. The next morning, however, there was a strong wind blowing from the southwest. After a big breakfast, we watched *Margo V* test the waters, so to speak, by venturing beyond the breakwater to see if we could proceed comfortably to Plattsburg. The bows of *Margo V* thrust up abruptly upon hitting the seas, revealing several feet of keel before she plunged her bow deeply into the next wave. Curiosity satisfied, *Margo V* returned to the anchorage.

Now we had a day to spend doing whatever seemed to be fun to do to fill in time. For instance, Ian rowed Mother over to the breakwater in our tender to check out the gulls. Our tender was actually a ten foot plywood Gremlin class Marconi cat-rigged sailing dinghy which was also very rowable. Like *Margo V* we towed our tender astern of us. This was generally a very satisfactory way of bringing a tender along on a cruise, except in a heavy following sea when the dinghy yawed a lot; or when the painter wrapped itself around the propeller when going in reverse in close waters.

The sailing gear for the Gremlin had been left at home due to lack of space aboard *Thalia Ann*. Using an oar as the mast, Ian fashioned out of a red and white checkered tablecloth a square-rigged sail and managed to sail the Gremlin downwind using the other oar as a rudder. Ian, my Mother and I rowed the dinghy ashore for supplies. The row back against the wind even in the lee of the breakwater proved very strenuous for Ian but we made it back in due course.

Dinny Fashioned two signal flags out of wash cloths and two files from the toolbox. She signaled Iris on board *Margo V* a happy birthday. Hugh signaled back with his regulation signal flags: "Thank you." When he was finished, Hugh continued with a project we learned he would do several times a summer, and that was to wet sand the mahogany superstructure of *Margo*.

Meanwhile back aboard *Thalia Ann* Barbie busied herself scrubbing the topsides which always managed to pick up scum at the waterline due to oil and other junk which one finds floating on the water surface in canals and harbours. Johnny Monroe on a mission to satisfy the continuing demand for ice for our ice boxes, finding no ice at Rouses Point, returned claiming he "stole" the supply from a local ice house.

Winds had been strong all afternoon. Then the wind dropped, followed by an exciting electrical storm. At 1800 hours our fleet of two moved to the mouth of a small creek for protection from shifting winds.

None of the weather changes stopped a young man fishing in a runabout with a buddy from taking my sister Diane to the movies as arranged earlier in the afternoon. He arrived back to pick her up just as the lightning storm was hitting our moorage. By evening, winds had returned to the west. At an appropriate time my sister also returned from her date.

The two cruisers rafted up again for the night and crews tried to sleep to the serenade of squeaking bumpers. However, before morning we cast off from each other thus swinging freely on our own anchors. This tactic eliminated bumper noise and provided for a more restful night.

The next day, as we organized ourselves for the run to Plattsburg, the sky to the south where we were bound looked very threatening even though we had a clear sky and westerly breeze. The barometer continued to drop. We weighed anchor at 0820 hours and without breakfast, got under way for Plattsburg. Then the skies started to look threatening again with rain squalls developing. We saw a bad one coming, crossing

Monty Bay into which we were enveloped with greatly reduced vision. However, by watching the stern of the *Margo V* and with one eye on the compass we progressed through the squall. Before long, the storm blew away before a strong westerly off Pointe aux Roches. Soon we came under the lee of Pointe aux Roches and were glad to round Cumberland Head and slip into the bay with Plattsburg in view just ahead.

The engine, after two to three running hours at maximum speed to cover the two dozen mile run, was starting to heat up and had reached 80 degrees Fahrenheit before Dad throttled down to 1200 from 1350 revolutions per minute. It seemed to be that at the higher revolutions the engine started to complain after running for two or more hours. A quart of oil every two hours seemed to be essential to keep *Thalia Ann* underway with surety.

At 1125 hours, we docked at Barkers behind the north end of the breakwater. We were all a little tired having had only bread and jam for breakfast while under way. Also, for those in charge of the boat on the trip, the weather had been rather unsettling and disturbing. Nevertheless, the motor and boat had acted beautifully. the skipper was elated that the engine on our *Thalia Ann* had survived the three hour run to Plattsburg through inclement weather. All went aboard *Margo V* to relax with conversation and refreshments. This was a busy harbour and other Lake St. Louis craft were seen, one a power boat and another a sailboat.

Plattsburg has always been a shopping destination for Canadians traveling by automobile from Montreal. This time, a group of our people who had come by boat went up shopping after lunch. They returned at 1500 hours, which gave my father and brother time to tidy up the ship.

Someone usually had to stay behind when the rest of the crew has shore leave. Dad and Ian swabbed decks and used liberal amounts of SABO cleanser in the forecastle where the head was located. SABO was a popular version of today's Ajax or Comet. Dad later relaxed after his efforts and demolished a bottle of cool Frontenac ale, another brand name of the times. By late afternoon Dad and Ian went into town to look around and eat a hotdog, which was an economic source of protein for us in those days.

That night, as at Chambly, winds were variable, such that for sleeping we went from dock to anchor behind the breakwater and back to the dock before settling for the night. At my age, the dock was always preferable, because confined on board at anchor was very boring. We did not even have a radio in those days.

Mother's hand must have been healing because on Friday morning she went uptown with Iris and Dodie Munroe to do some shopping.

Another event took place later that day. For sometime we have been watching for *Oracle* and phoning back to authorities and friends to ascertain the yacht's position along the route that we had followed but to no avail. We wanted to meet up with this third member of our little fleet before proceeding much further on the cruise.

Now, as mentioned before, *Oracle* was a forty-foot express cruiser with twin engine eight-cylinder engines. Skipper Don Thomson, an aircraft pilot as well, did not hesitate to use gasoline to get somewhere in a hurry when he wanted to do so. Later I saw Don's motion pictures of portions of their passage up the Richelieu River. The trees on the shore of the narrow river were fleeting by as if the Oracle was an automobile. We would later learn that this enormous hull with the bow up on a plane could kick up an enormous wake! The shoreline ecology of the Richelieu must have taken a real hit on that trip.

All that said, *Oracle* and crew appeared at noon with Don and his gorgeous redheaded wife Helen and six year old son Rusty, plus friends Ken and Vivien Place. They had left Lachine on Tuesday, July 29, having had to replace both port and starboard shafts and propellers before starting out. Now that we were all together the decision was made to set off for Stave Island about one hour's run from Plattsburg.

The three vessels set off at 1800 hours. Don Thomson, a big chap with an equally-sized sense of humour, proceeded to show off *Oracle's* new thrusting power by circling the other two boats kicking up an enormous wash. *Thalia Ann* tossed some, so in response Barbie waved my brother's Red Ryder air gun at *Oracle* which eventually resumed course for Stave Island.

Stave Island was a popular destination and there was a large craft with 'Camp-Fire' girls aboard made fast to the concrete pier on the north side of the island. We doubled up outside the pier with *Oracle*. Because our Primus stove was giving us some difficulty, a supper of fish and hamburgers was delayed. Eventually, with a full moon rising over the pine trees which circled our little harbour, the gang settled in the cockpit of *Thalia Ann* for an evening of conversation and listening to Don's portable radio. Before bedding down at 2330 hours some of the folks had a very cold swim. The air was cool too, so when Dinny chose to use the bunk at the after end of our cockpit she used four blankets.

Our first full day at Stave Island, Saturday August 1, started with a magnificent morning. The skipper and crew had a very cold pre-breakfast swim followed by coffee, porridge, which was regular fare every morning, and that other reliable to fill the stomachs of hungry young people, bread and jam.

My brother and I hiked up to and climbed a derelict forestry lookout tower which we had seen from the pier. Others went up later and took pictures of the harbour. Then Ian, Rusty and I picked raspberries for supper. We also checked out a boarded-up cottage and outbuilding not too far from the pier.

Although it was fun just to loaf around, there were sundry duties to perform such as laundry, miscellaneous repairs, cleaning and even hair washing. In those days unfortunately, the thought that soapsuds would contaminate the marine environment never crossed our minds. Meanwhile, aboard *Margo V* Hugh repaired the galley stove, while Don went around filming all the goings on.

At noon hour, we found that the water was much warmer than at breakfast time. With the boats now docked on the inside of the pier, we were able to dive from the outside of the dock where a swimming ladder was available. It was a grand place to swim and my father enthusiastically recorded that "this is the most beautiful, happiest day of the cruise so far – none of the reports of Stave Island were exaggerated but in truth they did not do it justice".

Another yacht, *Restless,* similar to *Margo V,* with the Stevens family on board, arrived all the way from their home port of Syracuse, New York, to enjoy Stave Island.

It was marvelous at Stave Island. Those on board *Thalia Ann* had not experienced such a vacation spot before. We would not enjoy such a location again until five years later when we cruised as a family aboard the forty-foot ketch *Alfredem* to the Thousand Islands.

From August 1 to August 7th, Stave Island became our pied à terre at Lake Champlain. Various trips were made usually by *Margo V* or *Oracle* as required but they returned to Stave Island.

There was quite a bit of running around up the shore and back down to the boats moored alongside the concrete wharf. *Thalia Ann* was up on the basin side of the pier with the bow pointed towards the little harbour entrance. This position conveniently brought the cockpit closer to the center of activity. As I came charging back to the boat that afternoon I leaped to go aboard *Thalia Ann* and fell into the drink and after sinking below the surface of the water rose to find the topside of the boat close aboard my face and the dock behind. Having been programmed that I was in imminent danger, I hollered out in surprise and panic: "Save me!" I was unceremoniously hauled out with everyone laughing not only at my dunking but my cry for assistance.

Late in the afternoon the *Gladys R*, a very shipshape motor vessel, arrived. The skipper was a Lieutenant Commander of the U.S. Navy based in the Pacific. He brought her along the outside of the dock very neatly, my father wrote, and promptly headed ashore to prepare barbeque chicken for supper for his boss and guests. They sat around in folding deckchairs. When their dinner was over they left the Lieutenant Commander to carry all the chairs back to their boat. This did not impress my father as the most democratic behaviour on the part of the crew of the *Gladys R.* Dad made some sarcastic remarks in his log. Looking back, however, it makes me wonder why the crew of the *Thalia Ann* did not lend that beleaguered man a hand with his chairs.

We enjoyed a supper of hot dogs cooked on the fire followed by apple sauce and biscuits and thereafter we had a song fest around the campfire. We all "crashed" at 2230 hours. Mother, Diane and Barbie slept on the grassy hillside near the pier wrapped in blankets.

On Monday, August 4th, we arose at 0730 and by 1050 hours we cast off for Mallett's Bay which was one and a half hours away. The weather was clear with a light wind from the south. Our destination was the Eureka Marine Company dock in the bay. There we picked up 26 U.S. gallons of gasoline and filled the water tank. Ice was available at the nearby stores where we planned to buy provisions. *Oracle* came along on the trip to meet Don's Mother and await some friends who were going to join *Oracle* for the cruise. Meanwhile, *Margo V* took Diane on a run to Burlington. *Restless* went south to Willsboro Bay where it was reported that there was a good anchorage in the extreme south end of the bay. Father considered going there but we ran out of time.

While at Eureka Marine, Mother had her first swim with her burned hand. A ladder at the dock facilitated accessing the water. The crews loafed and shopped in the afternoon until Don's friends arrived followed by the return of *Margo* at 2000 hours. Diane was thrilled with her purchases in Burlington as well as a beautiful blouse bought and given to her by Iris. The blouse would cause some tears later in the cruise. Finally we left the dock for the night and anchored in a bay near the yacht club in 36 feet of water.

On Tuesday, August 5 we awoke at 0800 hours to a clear calm morning with a light wind from the east which promised a hot day. After breakfast, the crew started grumbling about the day's plans, so we upped anchor and returned to the dock for ice. Some excitement was to follow that day.

Thalia Ann followed *Margo V* across Mallett's Bay but our engine was not running smoothly so we hailed *Margo* and headed back. The motor seemed to improve, so we started to follow *Margo* again. All of a sudden Ian smelled gasoline! Dad raised the engine hatch in the cockpit to find gasoline spurting in a stream straight up from a loose fitting on top of the fuel pump. Dad quickly switched off the flow of gas to the engine. The fitting was then tightened and some of the gasoline was removed from the bilge.

Ian had lowered the anchor with ninety feet of chain but the water was much too deep for the rope we had available. So Dad decided to start the engine and return to Eureka Marine. There was much concern about gasoline fumes in the bilge, which when ignited by a spark blow a yacht to pieces. The spark from starting an engine can do it! So Diane, Rusty and I were put aboard *Margo V*. Ian stayed up forward, while Dad nervously stood on the deck outboard of the cockpit near the control panel on the port side. He reached his hand around to the starboard side of the control panel where the new started button was placed. He pressed the starter but nothing happened, the engine would not turn over at all!

The anchor was raised while *Margo V* took us in tow back to Eureka Marine. Hugh helped the Eureka mechanic Russell take off the fuel pump. They found a washer to fit and replaced the pump but the engine still would not start.

After trying out a new battery and checking the solenoid, they decided that the problem must be the starter itself. Sure enough, the starter was malfunctioning. So, at 1600 hrs. the manager of the marina took the starter to Burlington. Even at that late time of the working day, he was back in one hour with the repaired starter. The device was quickly reinstalled and performed as it had never done before. All this work had been done for a total charge of ten dollars. Ironically, the starter was supposed to have been reconditioned and guaranteed for ten dollars the winter before by an outfit in Montreal which purportedly specialized in ignition systems. My father vowed to have a "chat" with them when he returned to Montreal.

Accompanied by *Margo V* we left the Eureka Marine right away and rejoined *Oracle* at Stave Island by 1930 hrs. Iris and Hugh were welcomed aboard our boat for a late dinner. Later that night Mom and Dad tried sleeping ashore but the night was warm and the mosquitos drove them back to the boat.

Wednesday, August 6th was another hot and sunny day spent in part washing clothing on the rocks, including underwear and pajamas which were "strewn all over the island." Everybody was in swimming intermittently all day long to keep cool.

Rusty Thomson, Ian and I took the Thomson's dinghy with an outboard around the island to check it out. The island was a little too large to venture about in a rowboat, and having an outboard was marvelous. The outboard complained a bit at first, so Don with his knowledge of motors, made a few adjustments and off we went!

The usual hi-jinks went on later in the day with an early cocktail hour. Dinny decided to show the adult gang her new blouse that Iris had bought for her at Burlington. She was devastated when someone accidently burned a hole in it with a cigarette. Nurses-in-training had no money for luxuries and now the blouse was ruined!

Just before supper my father decided to repair a leak in the head and found it a bigger job than anticipated. He did not complete the work until after dark. After I was settled in bed, Barbie dashed along the wharf as we were wont to do, and leaped aboard our boat. She frightfully impaled the heel of her foot on the erect spout of an oil can which had been left on the cockpit deck!

Once again, Hugh came over with his first aid kit. After a quick examination, I heard him joke out loud that what one needed to treat this wound was an ice pick. And of course that is exactly what he used, without my sister's realization, to open up the wound and apply hydrogen peroxide.

I suspect that the oil can may have been used to help repair the biffy or perhaps for engine repairs at Eureka Marine. For whatever reason, the oil can was not where it should have been. In any case, my father pointed out philosophically in his log that two lessons should be learned for cruising. "A place for everything and everything in its place" and "Do not run around after dark in bare feet!"

After Barbie awoke the next day, Thursday August 7th, Hugh came aboard and found that Barbie's foot was not infected and that her temperature was normal, so prompt treatment the night before precluded further complications. She was so well that she and Ian, with a blue sky overhead, went aboard *Oracle* for a run to Plattsburg for ice.

When *Oracle* returned, the Thomson's hosted a birthday party for Dad with dinner provided by *Margo V.* It must have been a good party because the whole ship's company retired early.

On Friday, August 8th, the time had come to start the trip for home. After a rainfall the night before, with the wind from the south, *Thalia Ann* and *Margo V* cast off for Plattsburg. *Oracle* had some vacation time left and had plans to proceed south to Willsboro Bay as recommended by the Stevens family at Stave Island.

After a good run under clear skies, we arrived at Plattsburg a couple of hours later with time for shopping uptown by the "girls" and lunch aboard ship. Departure for Rouses Point was at 1500 hrs. with arrival at 1830 hrs. During the trip the wind direction changed to blow freshly from the north near Isle la Motte. In the good-sized seas our cruiser performed admirably, although the engine started to heat up. Once again a quart of motor oil brought the engine temperature back to the normal 71 degrees F.

We anchored out from the town pier while Canada Customs officials came aboard for an uneventful inspection prior to re-entry into Canada. After supper on board we weighed anchor at 1930 hrs. for the short run to Lacolle, Quebec.

As it would happen, the inspectors were off duty by then. The skippers decided that it was too late to reach any other anchorage, so we tied up to the Customs wharf. A cool north wind was blowing which made our berth rather uncomfortable. Dad "kept anchor watch" and wandered around two or three times in the night checking lines and watching over the dinghy. The night was noisy as well as cool because automobiles ran over loose planks on a nearby bridge and waves sloshed against pilings and the concrete wharf.

Saturday, August 9 saw Dad up at 0600 hrs., followed by Diane at 0730 hrs. on a cool but sunny day. Diane took a swim off the wharf, much to the pleasure of some local admirers. Planning to have breakfast underway, the *Thalia Ann* crew cast off in a hurry to get going and promptly forgot its manners.

We had forgotten that *Margo V* was now shorthanded since Johnny and Dede had left the cruise to go home on the train. It was a cuttingly sarcastic "Thank you" voiced by Iris busily handling lines by herself up on the dock that made us realize that we had committed a bad faux pas by not helping *Margo V* cast off. The silence in our cockpit was deafening and the looks of dismay on the faces of my parents were very disconcerting indeed. By then it was too late to make amends as the boats were underway and too far apart for voicing apologies. The run to St. Jean was a long, unhappy two hours and twenty minutes. No mention is made of the reunion which took place at the St. Jean canal bank except to say that Mother went on board *Margo V* to help with the docklines on our way through the canal later that day. Her burned fingers were no longer a problem.

While taking on gasoline at the canal side under the bridge, Hugh dropped his gas tank cap overboard. Ian dove down but could not find it. It would not be Ian's last dive into murky canal waters on this trip. However, Hugh put on his special underwater lenses and brought up the gas cap first try.

Before we left Saint John at 1330 hrs., Dad went up to the local Canada Life office for some much needed cash. There were no credit cards in those days. At the same time Dinny phoned her future fiancé, Art Walter, in Montreal to come over and meet us at Chambly later in the day. We made the port of Chambly at 1545 hrs. and Art joined us an hour later. Hugh and Iris came aboard *Thalia Ann* for dinner.

The afternoon had become overcast with a north wind blowing. We were permitted by the lockmaster to lie on the west side of the pier, which was quite comfortable. While chatting with the lockmaster, he warned us that the Ste. Ours lock was not open to pleasurecraft on Sunday! As we were unable to reach the lockmaster at Ste. Ours to confirm this information, the skipper went to bed with a feeling of uncertainty about this potential delay in our return home and the consequences of returning a day late back to the office.

On Sunday, August 10, the sky had cleared when we arose at 0830 hrs. Dad tried to telephone Ste. Ours again but with no luck. The two skippers decided to carry on anyway. Art was able to catch the noon train back to Montreal and we had time to go over the engine as to battery strength, engine oil and grease caps before leaving Chambly finally at 1050 hrs.

After all the concern about locking through at Ste. Ours, we found that the lock was open for business! So we cleared Ste. Ours at 1445 hrs. and Sorel at 1620 hrs. With a clear sky overhead and *Margo V* a one-half mile ahead of us, we proceeded to Ste. Sulpice and arrived at the jetty at 2016 hrs, just before dark, having had supper underway. My father and I checked out the village that evening but everyone else was tired, such that we all went to sleep at 2200 hrs. on a very calm and quiet night.

On Monday, August 11, we had to make it back to PCYC so that Hugh and my father could get to the office on Tuesday morning. Nevertheless, time was taken to go uptown after breakfast for milk, bread and oil for our chronically thirsty motor. While the ladies did the shopping, my father and I investigated the local hotel which strangely had caged monkeys in the hotel garden. Meanwhile, Ian and Hugh worked on and improved the sound of our vessel's horn which might prove very useful on our trip upcurrent through the busy port of Montreal and the Lachine canal.

The sky was blue but the visibility with a westerly breeze was somewhat hazy when we left Ste. Sulpice at 1100 hrs. By 1300 hrs., we were at the western end of Isle Ste. Therese and we could see Pointe aux Trembles at the eastern shore of Montreal island. We continued to follow *Margo V,* which in turn was following a steamer. At that time Diane and I were aboard *Margo V.*

Back on *Thalia Ann*, the steering was becoming more difficult as the river current increased in strength. A large freighter called the *City of Carlyle* in passing produced a large stern wave which we had to plunge through bow on as she headed downstream. My father commented that he was glad it was not the *Queen Mary* going by.

We reached Longue Pointe at 1415 hrs. It was a long disheartening slog up the Ste. Mary's current at a net speed over ground of one knot.

Since *Thalia Ann* had a maximum through water performance of seven knots, that was some current. There was a great sigh of relief when we all pulled into Victoria Basin underneath Black's Bridge. At the Victoria Basin pier we saw the *Moosemin* tied up there with Corporal Ray Cassidy cheerily waving us on.

We proceeded through the first two locks of the Lachine Canal with ease and a crust of dirt all over the boat. Filth was a fact of life in this section of the Montreal waterfront, both in the air and on the water.

Suddenly, we lost forward power and it felt like the engine propeller had dropped off. Ian went overside into that garbage-filled canal water but found nothing out of order. Hugh had to come back and tow *Thalia Ann* into Keating's pier. Then Hugh himself went overboard with his goggles and immediately realized that the propeller shaft had backed out of the coupling of the engine. He had warned my father of this possibility some time previously because he had noted that there was only one pin holding the coupling in place. With Hugh's guidance the coupling was successfully reassembled.

We left Keating's at 1840 hrs. and pushed on, finally stopping at the pier on the western end of the canal for a quick supper and departure at 2100 hrs., to work our way up through Lake Ste. Louis to PCYC. Without any warning we were engulfed by a plague of shad flies that covered both boat and crew. Shad flies are a fact of life on Lake Ste. Louis but this fog of flies was more than we had ever experienced before and was most unpleasant.

Back on Lake Ste. Louis we were finally able to pick out the red spar in the Dorval channel. We were in home waters and easily proceeded up through the brown water of the north side channel of the lake and docked at PCYC at 2216 hrs.

Dad logged that the trip had been a "most interesting, healthy and enjoyable cruise." He had "gained a great deal of experience in what was really a somewhat ambitious trip for our first real cruise."

In 1950 my father had bought his first post-war automobile.

The future would bring the family many more cars and a variety of boats and boating activities. Nothing, however, would match the excitement and fun of that cruise to Lake Champlain on the *Thalia Ann*.

Thalia Ann with family and friends aboard

David

As the Wind Blows

The wheel turns
from left to right.

The wind is blowing
just,…..just right.

The boat will tack,
turn to the right.

It is a red sky,
a red sky at night!
It is a sailor's delite,

For if it was to be
red sky in the morning,
it would be a sailor's
Warning!

Barbara: Ian

ONE

He died last spring. His name was Ian, and he was my brother.

I had known his disease was in its final stages when I saw him in August and should have been prepared for the news, but I was not. When he had shown such incredible determination by coming to the enchanted lake to see us again, perhaps we began to believe he was invincible.

Coming to terms with my distress took a long time and at some point I decided to try a re-reading of our correspondence and see if it would help. Ian had lived in England for many years and I lived in Canada, but the distance hadn't mattered with trips home and letters bridging the gap. Re-reading the letters and reliving our shared experiences calmed me somewhat, enough to begin an essay about him.

My jottings and later discussions with his wife and sons soon stimulated a broader concept, and, as I worked, the healing process began. The bond between us had been very strong and it almost seemed as though he was lending me strength with my new and larger project.

Barbie & Ian - 1935

Ian was the third of four children born during the Depression to a Lakeshore family whose father had a steady job but very small income.

A sturdy, sober little boy, he was a great foil for his mercurial sister. I could make him laugh and it was always great fun to watch his eyes twinkle when he saw the humour in my comments. Being the middle two children, perhaps our special relationship had begun early, as we struggled to understand our place in the family structure. He was the first son, and was required to shoulder specific family responsibilities at an early age. I was older, but tiny in stature, and he felt, I suppose, that he had to take care of his 'little sister'.

Blunt in his conversation, and occasionally very sarcastic, his words stung me sometimes, but being three years older, I comforted myself with the knowledge he would understand when he faced similar problems. He caught up with me soon enough and the warmth of shared amusement over our early ignorance forged even closer bonds. We were far from perfect but we learned to appreciate each other and overlook the occasional blunder.

In 1937, the last child in the family was born and we also gained a mother's helper from New Brunswick. Dorothy Magee was a wonderful addition to the family and carried the baby along with her while she oversaw our myriad activities. We loved her for her tenderness with the baby and her kindness to the rest of us.

When the depression waned and the war started Ian helped a patriotic neighbour mix cement for a flagpole base, writing his initials in the cement before it dried. When Harry Crombie died, the flagpole was gifted to Ian who proudly raised the ensign each morning. The flagpole came with us every time we moved and I last saw it on the hill at The Three Pines, Dad's house near Sutton.

All the village children were affected by the strange, frightening wartime events and unfamiliar restrictions. We soon learned to either use our imaginations or do without. "Making do" was a term we came to understand very well as we adjusted to what we considered tough Canadian rationing rules and regulations.

Certain foods were rationed, others were unavailable, and since our Mother was blessed with a family whose children all had a sweet tooth, she too had to learn the art of creatively stretching sugar, jam and butter allotments.

The four of us were initiated into the intricacies of dismembering chicken wings and necks as our share of the bird, and were sprinkling dried grass on our vegetables which Dad felt had enormous nutritional value. After eating that disgusting mix, desserts of coarse brown bread and molasses were ambrosia!

We didn't eat the two-pound pike that Ian caught one day but I can clearly remember that we ate bony perch fished from Lake St. Louis and voted against eating the tiny ducks that, until they were cleaned and roasted, had been freezing on the clothes line off the back porch.

New clothes were a luxury our parents couldn't afford, and at times we looked very shabby. But we didn't care. How we looked was unimportant when we were always outdoors with so many wonderful games to play. Anyway, all our friends looked just as shabby as we did and sartorial splendor waited until we were older and could afford such luxury. The boys wore breeks for years, a type of heavy trousers, wide at the hips and narrow at the knees. Large leather knee patches sometimes met with coarse woolen kneesocks, but often they simply slipped apart and were left that way or were rolled down to their ankles.

None of us had any money to spend and very little to spend it on, other than the infrequent treat of an ice cream cone or a bag of delicious hot, greasy and forbidden French fries. Ian's favourite was the one-cent candy we purchased at Mireault's store in the village when we were lucky enough to receive some coin from an adult, and the new rich Mello Roll ice cream cylinders which were wrapped in cardboard at the factory and put into a crispy new biscuit-type cone when ordered at the store. This new ice cream was expensive and wasn't purchased very often, but the thick creamy flavours were terrific and are still remembered by us all.

Dad somehow managed to get us a six-seater toboggan and we flew down the steep hill on the south side of Beaconsfield golf course with our friends, taking turns at being captain of the ship holding tightly onto the rope at the front. I have a picture of Ian captaining a crew of neighbourhood children when he was hardly old enough or strong enough to do the job. He appears to be about six years old, and as I remember did a credible turn as captain.

We learned to ski, first on the gentler north slope of the club and later on the suicide run wearing secondhand skis Dad had found for us. We played a tough game of skinny at Clearpoint skating rink, and, when we were invited, skated as gracefully as we could to Strauss waltzes at the French rink in the village. It must have been a challenging trading task for Dad to keep four children supplied with useable secondhand sports equipment. The skates often had to be supplemented with newspapers or thick socks to achieve a reasonable fit. Ski repairs were frequent and with the rest of us Ian learned to sew leather straps, make new boot laces from scrap leather and apply coat after coat of boot dubbin and ski wax to our precious possessions.

As war casualty lists lengthened, we spent evenings together listening to "L for Lanky" on the radio, applauding Curly the bomb aimer and the crew's narrow escapes from enemy fire, and had nightmares after listening to the cruelty described on the program "Song of Norway". We listened to the nightly news with our parents and never missed a Churchill or Roosevelt broadcast. To soothe our spirits once a week we tuned into the Metropolitan Opera on Saturday afternoon and the Church in the Wildwood, fifteen minutes of church hymns on Sunday.

We shared the enormous excitement when a plane crash-landed behind our school, dashing across the fields during recess to see the results and speculated between ourselves about the possibility of sabotage and the fifth column. When one of our local fliers was killed flying over Lake St. Louis the speculation grew even stronger.

In the summer, we scuffed our shoes at the baseball diamond in Larocque Park as well as at school, and served our sailing apprenticeship at the yacht club. These activities were all free and active children took advantage of them.

Sometimes our neighbourhood game of run-sheep-run or baseball could end abruptly with the wail of the 9 o'clock siren reminding us of the time. The strict curfew hour for those under 16 had once again been announced! I can also remember my embarrassment when I was stopped by the local constabulary because my skirt length did not meet with the municipal by-law. I had to go home and put on a garment that covered my knees.

On cold winter mornings, when the walk to school seemed endless, Mother popped a dried prune into each young mouth hoping the chewing movement would prevent frostbite, at least on our faces. Gum would probably have worked as well, but who could afford gum?

Big snow forts were built at each corner of the driveway as soon as we had enough snow and we had marvelous snowball wars with the other kids, developing good throwing arms and accuracy.

We learned how to use coal sparingly by watching Dad attend to the furnace and jacket heater, and to dry our winter clothing on the radiators. The smell of wet wool mitts on a hot radiator is a childhood memory that is hard to forget!

When Mother cooked the ingredients for crocks of marmalade, mustard pickles and cookies at Christmastime, we helped to peel, chop and sort fruit and vegetables. Earthenware crocks of these goodies were stored in the pantry off the kitchen, where, on occasion, we would liberate delicious ice-cold ginger cookies. My own children later experience the same delight when they liberated ginger cookies from the freezer.

I must admit here that we were very pleased when a real refrigerator eventually arrived to replace our leaky ice box after the war, and when our huge wood/coal-fired, dirt-producing stove was removed to make room for a shiny all-electric stove.

We may have lacked certain creature comforts in the war years, but we were enriched in other ways.

One way we learned about the world was from the assortment of visitors who shared our simple meals. There were submarine and ship commanders, army officers and fliers, all on leave from their wartime duties, and all from different backgrounds and peacetime occupations. We listened intently to their stories, while obeying the parental dictum "Children should be seen and not heard." After the conflict came to an end it was former prisoners of war who came to our dinner table and enlightened us about a grim aspect of war.

The storytellers had another thing in common, though, and that was their enjoyment of sailing and the desire to talk about it. It was fascinating fare and there was one youngster in particular, Ian, who listened to every word!

As soon as we were old enough, we delivered newspapers, caddied at the golf club, ran messages, cut lawns (with the old and cumbersome push mower) and took care of neighbourhood children to earn precious pennies.

Resentful of restriction, we learned when to speak up and how to keep our own counsel. We joined local youth groups and absorbed their ideas on familial duty.

We squabbled over family chores and sweated over our homework, and in spite of a somewhat dysfunctional family life, or maybe because of it, we received a reasonably good education and developed strong healthy bodies. We won sports and academic awards and entered adulthood fairly well prepared.

Were we all successful? Depends on your point of view and value system. The four of us had developed an attitude towards life that was shaped, inevitably I suppose, by the informality of our life on the water, as well as the lingering impact of the depression and war.

We had slowly become aware of our personal skills and gained valuable experience as we tried to attain our goals. We did our best to treat others as we wished to be treated, were honest to the core, and the accumulation of possessions was never a first priority. We survived the usual life challenges and lived quiet, unremarkable lives.

Ian, who had always loved unusual challenges, enriched his life with extraordinary sailing adventures and world-wide vacation treks. I still have postcards he sent me from places we used to consider very exotic, such as Bali, Morocco, Antigua, South Africa, Lapland, and the Canary Islands.

His sea voyages always intrigued me, since I am not a courageous sort and prefer my adventures on the pages of a book. Part of this project presents stories he wrote about two long cruises aboard his beloved sailboat *Bente*, which I had read years ago and which I thoroughly enjoyed re-reading. Perhaps you will, too!

Discovering *Bente* in a Northern England farmyard was the realization of Ian's lifelong dream to own a large cruising sailboat, although it took five years of hard work for him to reconstruct and rig her to his ever-exacting standards.

Ian's first story began on a late summer evening in Weybridge, Surrey…

Ian

TWO

It was an ad in the P.B.O. that caught my eye like a friend's face in a crowd.

After countless months of dreaming the impossible and browsing aimlessly through the small ads of yachting magazines, here suddenly was a flicker of hope …

35 FT NORWEGIAN TUMLARE STYLE CUTTER.

FIRE DAMAGED HULL. SUITABLE FOR

REPAIR OR G.R.P. PLUG £500 PENRITH

Several days of unanswered phone calls, and finally the inevitable "… Well someone local is interested, but if you hurry …'"

It being only a week before start of Michaelmas term the boys, aged 13 and 10, were eager for any diversion and with mother away visiting relatives a quick trip to Cumbria to look at a boat had a touch of intrigue.

The monotonous 5 ½ hour drive from Weybridge sharpened our anticipation and finally, in a farmyard nestled in the empty rolling hills of Cumbria perched *Bente*, looking very out of place and disheveled, but somehow proud and defiant.

Standing on her 5' – 9" draught in her cradle, *Bente* towered over us, and the boys' excitement overcame them,

'Wow, Dad, are you going to buy it?'

I suppose I already knew because the beautiful lines of sheer, stem, and turn of bilge were irresistible, but the boys understood when I explained that major decisions required careful calculation, so the survey of boat and damage began.

Close seamed Norwegian pine planking on oak ribs at 9" centres, copper nails and bronze screws fastened, with a massive 3 ton cast iron keel and glass fibre sheathing up to the waterline. A good start.

Inside, the fire which had spread from the adjacent cruiser in a boatyard had completely destroyed the cockpit, half the cabin and decking, and left badly scorched many of the ribs and areas of planking, but fortunately above the waterline.

The internal fitments and engine had all been removed which at least had facilitated examination.

Having read with interest some articles on the new West epoxy sealing and glueing of timber construction I thought that *Bente* was reparable, if only for rather limited usage.

After an understandably one-sided discussion of terms of sale, not only was it agreed to pay full asking price for the hull but, after some quick mental calculations involving insurance policies and bank managers, to throw in a second £500 for the remains of equipment and sails.

Enlisting the vendor's help to arrange for a crane and transport, the car boot was loaded with our new found gear and the boys and I headed home full of happiness and pride.

Some cheerful staff in a motorway restaurant helped us with our celebratory dinner and the hamburgers pretended to be filet mignon.

There was a data sheet left over from the previous sale which described *Bente* as being designed by A. Holth and built by Iverson at Skjeberg, Norway in 1945.

We couldn't wait to tell our Norwegian friends, who had been our neighbours in Weybridge until their recall the year before, but what a delightful surprise when Mari told us that her maiden name was Iverson, the builder was her uncle, and Skjeberg was the coastal village which had been the family summer home for generations.

Here an idea was born. Would it be possible to have a reunion with these friends by sea and take *Bente* home?

We had for many years been spending our summers on the west coast of Sweden north of Gothenberg with my wife's foster parents and knew this area to be one of the finest sailing and cruising areas in the world.

The projected construction gained a new dimension and motive.

Later, on a bright Saturday in mid-October a cradle sat ready in the front of the Weybridge garden, fortunately more than an acre, and a few friends had been drawn to the occasion.

A roar of engines and a mobile 25-ton crane and boat transporter came up the chestnut lined avenue – the excitement was nearly impossible to contain.

There was an hour of feverish work of guiding her into the makeshift cradle, built on very vague recollections of hull shape. The transporters had the sense to insist that the lifting straps be provided with a thwart to protect hull shape during lifting and I was grateful for the experienced advice.

The rebuilding job lay ahead but nothing could dampen the joyful excitement of *Bente's* arrival into our front garden, not even the unhappy dismay of the one neighbour who could see her from his garden.

The first order was to construct a working cover, and this was a pitched roof frame erected from ground and secured to the cradle, and covered by clear plastic sheeting from the D.I.Y.

Then came removal of the charred and irreparable cabin and decking, and placement of temporary lateral thwarts to maintain hull shape.

The bilges were full of debris with melted drippings from the plastic cover acting as a binder. Fortunately there were no unexpected discoveries and *Bente* was rot free.

With all the other usual family and job demands on time it took many months to splice in new sections to 42 ribs, a new section of bilge stringer, and complete new beam shelf.

What a pleasure though to be now building back, and using sweet new white oak for ribs, BC fir for shelves, and mahogany for deck beams. Bulkheads from five eighths ply were introduced instead of the original frames.

The following summer afforded the warm dry conditions to finish stripping the hull to bare wood inside and out and treating with West epoxy formulation. It was our luck that her planking had been well seasoned before building and there was no cracking.

There was just enough time during the following autumn and spring to install deck beams before being interrupted by a house move in summer of 1980, and the necessity of relocating our little boatyard, as the new front garden surely wasn't intended for 35-foot yachts. A majestic beech tree stood guard.

Some carefully paced discussions over a period of weeks with Terry, the proprietor of Weybridge Marine, finally concluded that a corner of the car parking area could be used by a boat arriving by road instead of the river. Then another manoeuver with crane and transporter through Weybridge town, and again without incident.

It was a lovely spot sitting with the bow stuck out over the River Wey, just at the confluence with the Thames, but there were many distractions from activities on the Thames, as well as curious passers-by on the road, plus all the motor cruiser folk of the boatyard.

They didn't take us very seriously at first – the huge keel itself saw to that – but as work progressed some of them were very kind with advice and help, and finally accepted me into their Sunday lunch drinking circle at the nearby pub.

Building an extension to the house in summer 1981 interrupted boat progress which did not really resume until mid-1982. Then cabin trunk was installed and interior largely roughed out.

Early spring 1983 saw frenzied progress toward a hoped-for summer launch. Water and fuel tanks were created in stainless by the foreman of a local appliance manufacturer, and a new marinized Kubota engine was acquired, again through an ad in P.B.O., from a chap up near Newcastle who took over the stock of Hydromarine, Ireland, when it went bankrupt in the late 1970's.

Terry remembered a local farmer friend who had a high fork lift to place the engine on the bridge deck, and then with a borrowed cable winch and pipework horse straddling the main hatch it was lowered into place remarkably easily.

Preparing the engine bed and positioning the vibration mounts had taken much longer!

A very hectic day at the Beaulieu Boat Jumble for the third year running (as both seller and buyer) provided a nearly new matching set of 7 upholstered mattresses that could be easily adapted to our 5 berths plus 2 saloon back rests, for a tiny fraction of cost to make, and from the same vendor came a pair of winches to replace a fire damaged pair.

The boys proved to be tireless bargain scouts among the many hundreds of jumble sellers and came up with paint, fittings, and useful sailing gear.

Further guidance from sympathetic staff at a chandlery in Holborn provided good value in toilet, stove (2 burner paraffin), navigation lights and much more.

Construction proceeded smoothly through cockpit, hatches, gunwales, deck fittings and finishing off down below, but suddenly it was deep into summer and plans had to be revised to an autumn launch, and a winter of working up and rigging.

When in September all was ready to take to water, the river Wey offered no more than 3'6" of depth over the bar at its mouth so back to crane and transporter again for a transfer to the south coast, instead of the dreamed about triumphant trip down the Thames.

The initial launching was shattered by the discovery of a mini fountain from the cooling water inlet – the only hull fitting not replaced – which had succumbed to electrolysis. Fortunately my understanding wife and the crane operator were the only witnesses to my folly.

But then afloat she was a pretty sight, sitting pertly well above her waterline.

Arrangements had been made for a swinging mooring in Portsmouth harbour – which proved to be an unhappy choice.

The long trips by car to the coast, plus the restrictive timetable of the ferry launch and some very stormy weekends, combined for a miserable winter, only slightly softened by the fascination of maritime Portsmouth harbour.

John Boyce was a very patient consultant on choice of spars and rig using my amateurish sketch of the original, based on measuring the sails and the burned pieces of mast out on the front lawn.

Supposedly, the narrow 8'6" beam preferred a double spreader rig and I tentatively dispensed with the original running backstays in favour of fixing them permanently as far aft as reasonable boom travel would allow. With both fore and aft lowers it was a generous rig.

Then a super father and son team from Solent Rigging brought their swagging equipment alongside Gosport Boatyard and *Bente* was transformed in one day from a hull to a full sailing ship.

What a lift to morale after the long winter, and relief that everything fitted. She was a very rewarding sight.

April passed and with it my 50th birthday. The idea to sail to Norway had matured into a plan and now absolute determination set in.

It would be *this* year.

Weather conditions in the Swedish west coast and Oslo fjord become rather more windy as August comes, so the best departure would be during July.

Sails were hung, leads positioned, winches mounted and hundreds of little jobs done. The Sestrel Moore compass which came with the boat was restored by caring people at the east London factory, and boxed by an expert of their recommendation. Mounting it on the main sliding hatch on a removable bracket proved to be a great success.

B & G had overhauled the Hecta echo sounder and supplied a second hand mounting plate so the second most important piece of navigation equipment was installed and ready.

Charts were acquired and some rough calculations suggested a trip of about a week give or take a day or two either through the Kiel Canal or outside Denmark.

It was decided to employ a professional skipper as a life of sailing primarily on inland waters and not having had time to do more than the RYA competent crew course as a refresher was no way adequate for such a trip. John Kitchen was volunteered by his wife over the telephone and in late June we met on board alongside the yard.

His checklist identified the necessity for a bosun's chair, reef points in the main, and extra fuel storage, and in the event they were all necessary, especially the reefs. It was agreed that John was the boss at sea but the trip was to be viewed as a holiday and not just a passage, so he would accede to requests as to timing and routing.

Departure was set for July 21 by which time the boys would be out of school and it left some precious weekends to finish preparations.

Our eldest son had planned to crew but the temptation of southern Spain with his friends overcame him and crewing arrangements became a bit complicated.

Friends and relatives appreciated the invitation but none seemed able to make the trip. One wondered.

Finally an adventure-loving friend noted for camel safaris in Africa persuaded himself that after building and sailing a Mirror, that was a good next step. Thus we were 3 with John W to go with John K and one or two possibles for a fourth.

Saturday the 21st found us at Safeway at 8.00 am to top up with provisions, and by 11.00 am, I was up the mast fitting the radar reflector.

The last few days we were moored alongside at Campers and that was a great help.

John phoned to elect a 6.00 pm departure based on wind and tide conditions – this gave a few more precious hours.

Friends arrived at midday for a send off and fortunately the afternoon was sunny and warm. They spent it in best yachting style, complete with a bit of bon-voyage bubbly provided by staff at the office.

By 5.00 pm anything left could be done at sea, and a quick trip to the fuelling barge made us ready in all respects.

Right on time John K arrived and with no further ado instructed us to cast off.

Except for some motoring to and fro in Portsmouth harbour this was *Bente's* maiden voyage – a big step if you will, but testing and preparation had allowed for that and our route would pass many ports well equipped with yacht services.

Sails were hoisted into a light south westerly on-shore evening breeze and John K set up the watches; 3 hours on and 6 off, with John W restricted to daylight watches at least at first.

Other assignments and responsibilities were quickly run through and then after a long hectic day thoughts could turn to a drink, to food, and to the joy of being at sea.

Routine set in immediately and with about 20 hours of engine assistance the variable SW and westerly breezes pushed us along past Worthing and Brighton.

Gradually the breeze came out of the east with some northing, so we tacked the long way around Dungeness Power Station from well in the bay, and then up toward Dover where we arrived to the South Goodwin early Tuesday morning under power, with a little help from a light northerly breeze.

The engine took us smartly across the first traffic separation land and John decided to take the route up the middle.

By Tuesday night the wind was up to force 5 locally, 6 on the nose from the north east down a ridge of high pressure, and we shortened sail to staysail and one reef, then two reefs, then we just rode the sea under staysail alone for the rest of the night.

The early morning weather forecast was for more of the same so in the spirit of holiday and out of respect for the mature years of *Bente* we headed for the Belgian coast some 6 hours away with double-reefed main and staysail on a beam reach.

The decision made, spirits lifted, and by late morning we reached a lee toward Flushing, and with help from a fisherman as we closed the coast, we happily discovered the super haven of Blankenberg, with its long breakwaters drawing us into a huge basin right in the heart of this holiday town.

Bente had passed an important test with flying colours and the motion at sea was all one could hope for. She was also remarkably dry, which rewarded the care taken to keep weight out of her ends. The only breakage was an original bronze jib fairlead which had suffered a crack propagated from a thread.

We spent two very enjoyable days there as the strong northeasterly swept down the coast and kept all the vacationers off the wide exposed beaches.

Super seafood restaurants and excellent wines and most of all two good night's sleep after jolly evenings talking exploits with neighbours from all over Europe en route up or down the coast – but all sheltering. A few odd jobs by way of improvements to in reefing gear, included roving a topping lift which had been overlooked somehow (rather useful for reefing John W said with a grin as he went up in the bosun's chair).

By Thursday morning the forecast was for winds to start moving into the north and then west, still strong but not quite on the nose.

A little trouble persuading the folding propeller to open in forward (I insisted on fitting one against all advice because I wanted a fast sailer) had us backing most of the way out of the harbour as our new found friends looked on in some wonder about our fate on the North Sea.

With 2 reefs, staysail and engine we struck out north west and gradually the seas became easier as we left the coastal shallows behind.

After an afternoon and evening of long tacking north off the Belgian and Dutch coasts, we fetched the Texel light vessel and could then lay our course close-hauled on port. We had a magnificent sail with the wind gradually pulling aft into the west as we eased slightly more to the east running down past the buoys off the Friesian Islands.

Our Wasp trailing log performed beautifully the whole trip, so who could deny John W's claim of 9K riding down a wave?

By keeping just shoreward of the string of marks we could watch passing shipping with more casual interest than in the English Channel. We opted to go via the Kiel Canal route instead of outside Denmark.

The course became more congested as we approached the Elbe estuary Saturday afternoon, but with an easing westerly we full sailed and motored on a flood tide up the Elbe and managed a carefully mentally-rehearsed but across the end of the 4-knot flood tide stream neatly into a crowded Cuxhaven yacht harbour at 0100 Sunday.

We were not much appreciated by the skipper of a very large German sailing yacht as we came alongside, but an apparently empty Dutch one next up the line offered no resistance.

Sleep came quickly, despite the lights and roaring trucks from the adjacent Ro Ro terminal, as we programmed ourselves to a 6 am start to get across into the Kiel Canal and hopefully through it as required in daylight.

Now totally confident in the faultless Kubota, which also pleased with a very low fuel consumption, we steamed the last of the ebb into slack water and arrived off the impressive canal entrance, then hovered around for a half hour or so with a small fleet of others waiting for the white 'come in' lights.

Quickly through the lock and hard to port into the yacht basin, where John W had to phone the Foreign Office to see whether an extra couple of days holiday would be possible.

As luck would have it, he was needed back as soon as possible, so he obtained information on rail connections to Hamburg airport and we were obliged to drop him off at a ferry landing some 15 kilometres along the canal.

It was a sad parting (the more so for him as he ended up carrying his bags some 3 miles to the railway station), and, in the peace of the canal, we had no thought yet for the chore of watch keeping 3 hours on and 3 hours off in the Baltic.

The pastoral scenery complete with farm boys waving our red ensign on its way was contrasted by the huge ships passing us, fortunately mostly in the opposite direction.

A convenient fuel dock prompted a stop late evening and we were warned to berth for the night as transit after dark is prohibited. Turning up a little river found us a yacht club and even an opening in the row of bow on moorings between posts. A hot shower in the tiny but well equipped clubhouse was most welcome.

John K phoned home to wish his wife a happy birthday and learned that the return delivery of a boat from Vindon, Sweden, just north of Gothenberg, had finally been confirmed. A planned 6 a.m. start was advanced by a bedlam of quacking about 3 a.m., but as we left the river and rejoined the main canal the turning buoy was marked Eider #1 in explanation.

By mid morning we were through into the Baltic and after a quick stop alongside the canal approach for fresh bread (no Danish pastry yet) we set off into the summer vacationland of the Baltic.

A light breeze from the east under a clear sky soon had us setting Yankee and full main on a northerly course into the Danish islands.

By evening the breeze had increased so we changed down headsails. Gradually the 3 on, 3 off watchkeeping organized us into a no-nonsense programme of sails and navigation.

As night fell the wind increased to SW force 4/5 so back in went the reefs. Food making became more and more basic and lack of sleep took its toll, but the spirit of fun and adventure did not wane.

Tuesday provided another exciting day of sailing with winds 5, locally 6, but thankfully from astern. By 1800 we closed a marker which proved to be just south of the Gothenberg estuary so from there we could hop the row of lighthouses up the coast toward our destination of Lysekil.

At midnight we were off Gulhomen lighthouse and idled our time till daybreak before entering the inside passage. Lightning flashes to the north added a touch of excitement as the breeze died away.

As soon as one could really say it was dawn, about 2.45 a.m., we headed in and after a majestic run through the rocky islands in the early morning calm we entered Lysekil yacht harbour, our destination.

Ship was tidied, and after reporting to the nearby 'Toll Bureau' we enjoyed a short breakfast in the local cafeteria.

John K took the little ferry boat to Fiskebacksil from whence it would be only a 10km taxi ride to Vindon, where one of his regular crew would be waiting for him to take the new Vindon 45 back to England.

A phone call to my wife's Swedish relatives soon brought Gunne and Pele to "take the strain" and move *Bente* to Bohus Malmon, our summer holiday home.

We used the modern well equipped marina as our base and for the next 10 days or so with my wife and younger son, Alan, who had arrived the day after us by car.

We pottered around the islands with relatives and friends, including trips to the lovely harbours of Kungshamn and Smogen with their shrimp trawlers and attendant flocks of gulls.

The inside passage through the coastal islands is heavily traveled in season, but there are few visitors except for Norwegians and the occasional German boat.

It was, nonetheless, an amusing surprise when a passing Swede, upon spotting our ensign, broke into song with the chorus of 'Rule Britannia'.

Pele and Gunne agreed to make up the crew with Alan and me for the trip to Norway which would take about 2 relaxed days, the first part of it up the inside passage including the lovely Soten Canal.

After an overnight stop at the little fishing village of Steningsund, right on the passage, we finished the trip to Skjeberg on a pleasant sunny day with a variable light breeze from astern which gave us a chance to try the spinnaker.

We sailed right up to the summer cottage of our Norwegian friends and dropped the hook.

The log read just over 800 miles.

As the local press described it the next day:

"Bente hjemme igjen etter 40 harde ar"

"*Bente* Home Again After 40 Hard Years"

Mandag 13. augsust 1984

Utrolig båthistorie fra Skjeberg

«Bente» hjemme ig etter 40 harde år

AV PÅL NILSEN

Livet fører med seg de merkeligste historier. Det har familien Brænne fra Sarpsborg til fulle fått oppleve. Under sine 15 år i London ble de meget gode venner med sine daværende naboer, familien Robertson. I 1978, etter at den norske familien hadde flyttet hjem igjen, kjøpte Robertsons en utbrent seilbåt. Det skulle vise seg at denne båten var en av dem som ble bygget på Skjebergkilens Båtbyggeri for 40 år siden og eksportert til utlandet. Og mannen som eide båtbyggeriet, Einar Iversen, var vitterlig fru Mari Brænnes onkel....

Etter å ha brukt fem år på å bygge den totalt nedbrente båten opp igjen, kunne Ian Robertson bli skipper på egen båt. Og hva var vel mer naturlig enn å legge jomfruturen til Norge, Skjebergkilen og familien Brænnes hytte i Sildevika.

– «Bente» er helt fantastisk, sier Ian, og tenker da ikke på sin kone. «Bente» er nemlig båtens navn, et navn som sannsynligvis har vært på farkosten siden den ble bygget i 1945.

I LONDON

Brænnes og Robertsons var nærmeste naboer da begge familiene bodde i Weybridge, en forstad til London. Gunnar Brænne arbeidet i 15 år ved Borregaards London-kontor, og hadde naturligvis tatt med seg sin kone Mari og datteren Victoria. Ian Robertson kommer opprinnelig fra Canada, men også han arbeidet for sitt kanadiske firma i Englands hovedstad.

Ians kone, Oili, er født i Finland og oppvokst i Sverige. Sammen har de sønnen Alan.

De to familiene ble gode venner, og etter at Gunnar Brænne startet opp ved Borregaard i Sarpsborg for seks år siden, har deholdt kontakten. Gjentatte ganger har dereist på ferie sammen, og de

gjen

JOMFRUTUR

– Helt siden jeg kjøpte båten og ble oppmerksom på at den var bygget i Skjebergkilen, har det vært min drøm å seile den hit. Og «Bente» oppførte seg eksemplarisk på sin jomfrutur, selv om det var storm over Nordsjøen, sier skipper Ian. Med seg på turen hadde han to seilervenner, mens resten av familien kom med bil.

– Like etter at Robertsons hadde kjøpt den brente båten, ringte de til oss i Sarpsborg, forteller Gunnar Brænne. – Ian hadde ingen aning om at Skjeberg, som det sto i følgebrevet til båten, er navnet på kommunen hvor vi har hytte, og som han selv hadde besøkt. Stor var selvsagat forundringen også for oss, når vi fikk høre at båten var bygget ved Skjebergkilens Båtbyggeri.

Det var altså Mari Brænnes onkel, Einar Iversen, som eide dette båtbyggeriet som holdt til i Grimsenkilen. Det er bare laget fem båter av denne typen - en 34 fots slupp. To av dem ble eksportert til Nederland, mens de tre andre gikk til USA. Så kom altså den ene av dem tilbake til utgangspunktet.

FANTASTISK

Ian Robertson har lagt ned mange timers arbeid for å få bygget «Bente» opp igjen. Da han kjøpte båten, var det ikke stort mer enn selve formen igjen. Til og med 14 spanter måtte skiftes. Ian kjøpte båten for £1.000 (10.000 kroner) og har brukt £5.000 til å bygge den opp.

– Det var mye mer arbeide enn det jeg først hadde trodd, men nå, etter at jomfruturen er vel tilbakelagt, er alt slitet glemt. «Bente» er en fantastisk båt, og den strålende konstruksjonen gjør sitt til at hun er en drøm å seile. Det er også en drøm som er gått i oppfyllelse når jeg har tilbakelagt seileturen over til Norge, men hvem kunne vel trodd at «Bente» med denne turen kom tilbake til det sted hvor hun ble bygget for 40 år siden?

«Bente» ble eksportert fra Skjebergkilens Båtbyggeri i 1945. 40 år ett er hun tilbake igjen, med engelsk skipper.

Barbara

THREE

After reading Ian's story, I wondered how my brother had become so keen and confident a sailor that a 7-hour leg of a voyage could seem routine to him. To me, each minute of each hour must have been filled with the many activities that keep a skipper alert, his crew safe, and required a great deal of nautical skill.

Pausing to look back over his life, it became clear that he had been steadily adding to his repertoire of these skills ever since he learned at a very young age that sailing was so much fun.

His first experience with boats had been in his own backyard when as a tiny lad he watched his father scrape and repaint our dark green dinghy. Then, when Ian was four years old, Dad purchased *Curlew*, a 21-foot Marconi-rigged sloop.

Curlew was built in Nova Scotia and delivered locally by freighter, a huge excitement for the townspeople as well as the family. Although she was already rigged she still needed a cabin and various finishing touches to ready her for family sailing.

Ian accompanied his Dad as he attended to these chores and he was quickly infected with his father's joy of owning and preparing a boat to sail on Lake St. Louis. His small size was not a deterrent as the yacht club was an easy short walk from our house.

As the war years dragged on, he was initiated into the basics of sailing on Lake St. Louis, and learned how to be useful aboard *Curlew*.

When the war was over, the family graduated to a 30-foot Richardson-design cabin cruiser. Used as a harbour craft during the war, she had been at the bottom of the Sydney, Nova Scotia, harbour more than once.

The ice box had been used as a coal bin and *Thalia Ann* was generally in very poor shape.

We all participated in her reconstruction, learning to caulk, sand and paint the wooden hull; to meticulously sand and varnish the mahogany bright work; to splice and whip ropes; to scrub bilges and decks; to make zippered canvas cockpit curtains and to sew quilted coverlets using old blankets.

The result of all our work was an attractive comfortable family cruiser with sleeping accommodation for seven people. Once the rebuilt engine operated satisfactorily and repairs to the hull were deemed tight, we were launched.

Ian was taught *Thalia Ann's* operating eccentricities, and assisted his Dad when for several years we cruised in company with other families on Lake St. Louis, Lake of Two Mountains and Lake Champlain.

Active aboard ship as well as ashore during the day, we ate simple meals, slept well at night, and ended our summers tanned and refreshed.

In their spare time the boys honed their sailing skills by crewing and skippering for other boat owners in club races and Montreal area regattas.

Over four summers, Ian crewed and skippered in *Rebel*, a 19-foot P.C. Class sloop owned by Archie Currie, one of the best local sailors, who mentored Ian on the precisions of racing.

When Ian was only 16 he represented Canada at an international sailing meet, after achieving acclaim for his success in winning a series of competitions against other able sailors from Eastern Canada and the United States.

A quote from the *Lakeshore News* in the summer of 1950 reads:

"Robertson, by sailing consistently well and avoiding protests and jams, came out on top with the highest point score. He defeated such expert sailors as Pangman and Henderson of R.C.Y.C., Toronto; Clapp and Rae of Queen's City Y.C., Toronto; Hamilton and Whitehead of Royal St. Lawrence; Kirby and ..."

More publicity followed and while the first broad heading had proclaimed, "Ian Robertson of R.C.Y.C. Will Represent Canada," the next one, together with a picture of skipper Ian and his crew, read: "Lakeshore Team Represents Canada in Sailing Meet.

"Ian Robertson, of Pointe Claire Yacht Club, who won the individual point honours in last week's Junior International yacht series, has been chosen to carry Canada's honours in the Semi-Finals of the Sears cup Race at Marblehead, Mass., emblematic of Junior sailing supremacy on the North American continent.

"The Sears Cup Semi-Finals which will be raced the weekend of Aug. 19, will see teams from the Eastern Seaboard competing for the honour of meeting winners from other Sears Cup Semi-Finals being held across the U.S."

What still amazes me is the fact that Ian at 16 had never even seen the sea before, much less raced on her, and yet, off he went to compete against America's best junior sailors.

When asked why, he said, "Unless I try, I'll never know if I can do it!"

When *Thalia Ann* had to be sold so we could buy a house, a kindly friend came to our rescue and offered Dad the loan of his 40-foot ketch on the understanding that its yearly overhaul and general upkeep was our responsibility. Fortunately the arrangement appealed to Dad and for several years we were able to take marvelous cruises aboard *Alfredem*.

Ian, unable to resist the challenge of pitting his skills against new competitors, entered *Alfredem* in cruising class races. She was a beautiful sight with all her sails full and her bow slicing the water, but she was not that swift, and I don't recall that she ever won a race.

Ian was never idle, and he later purchased a Y-Flyer, a Jolly boat and an E class boat, racing successfully in all of them. He once winter-stored the mast of his boat in our basement in Scarborough, and in the spring we manoeuvered the *Big E's* tall spar carefully through the basement window, then helped Ian with the spring sanding and varnishing.

Ian took his engineering degree at McGill, joined their sailing club, and earned his military commission with the University Naval Training Division. He captained a landing craft during Canadian/American naval exercises at Norfolk, Virginia, one summer, but the Canadian boys don't remember a certain evening ashore with much pleasure.

They all landed in hospital with ptomaine poisoning. Ian told me later that he collapsed in a restaurant bathroom and woke up in hospital with a big red M painted on his forehead. Morphine, I guess.

When he was still based locally Ian helped his Dad rebuild an old wooden double-ended ketch, *Curlew II*, taught the first junior sailing classes at a local yacht club, and later held the post of harbourmaster at his home yacht club.

But his work soon took him to posts in Toronto, to London, back to Toronto and then to a permanent London post. Always busy, he renovated one Toronto house and refurbished two large cottages in the English countryside, traveled for his company and sailed competitively when he could.

An avid gardener, he enjoyed experimenting with plants to determine to his own satisfaction whether or not they were suited to the English climate. Some were and some were not, but Ian had satisfied his own curiosity.

Through all these years of transfer across the ocean he sailed and won races in a variety of boats on both inland lakes and on the sea, and had married in Finland and began raising his two sons.

He was very happy to have his own family and inwardly pleased he was able to provide them with a comfortable life. He was modest about his many accomplishments, but I kept records on his activities and all his letters in my family archives, and I knew how hard he had worked to achieve his goals.

In 1987 Ian's company magazine carried a feature article on his participation in the annual Mid-Atlantic race aboard *La Marotte.*

This 1700-mile race took 12 days and 9 hours from the start line at Rotterdam to the finish in the Azores. *La Marotte* achieved a first in its division and a first on corrected time! Ian was quoted: "With spinnakers flying," related Robertson, "the fleet ran up the coast to the famous town of Scheveningen, to get clear of the busy shipping lanes into Rotterdam and then crossed toward England before turning south for the 1700 miles to the finish at Punta Delgada."

"Dolphins were frequent visitors, and at night their phosphorus streaks, as they approached at high speed and then dived under the boat, were disturbingly torpedo-like," stated Robertson. "They seemed to know and enjoy their effect. Of the three whales sighted, all were at a safe distance but not so the bulk carrier, which came up from astern and offered to run us down."

Ian's search for *Bente* had begun when he was posted to England a second time, and finding her ultimately led to the series of expeditions in northern waters.

Ian's 1993 adventure skippering *Bente* to Sweden was nine years after he had first taken her back home to Norway where she had originally been built. Now beautifully finished and outfitted in his spare time, *Bente's* renaissance was complete.

This trip covered over 1600 miles and was, as he wrote in '94, "a cruise from Waldringfield on the river Deben in Suffolk to the west coast of Sweden in a 34.5-foot cutter.

"It was not an 'epic' voyage, but one which, relative to the experience of the skipper, was a challenge, and provided much pleasure, a little discomfort, and an occasional bit of drama."

Father and sons check the keel

Bente with spinnaker

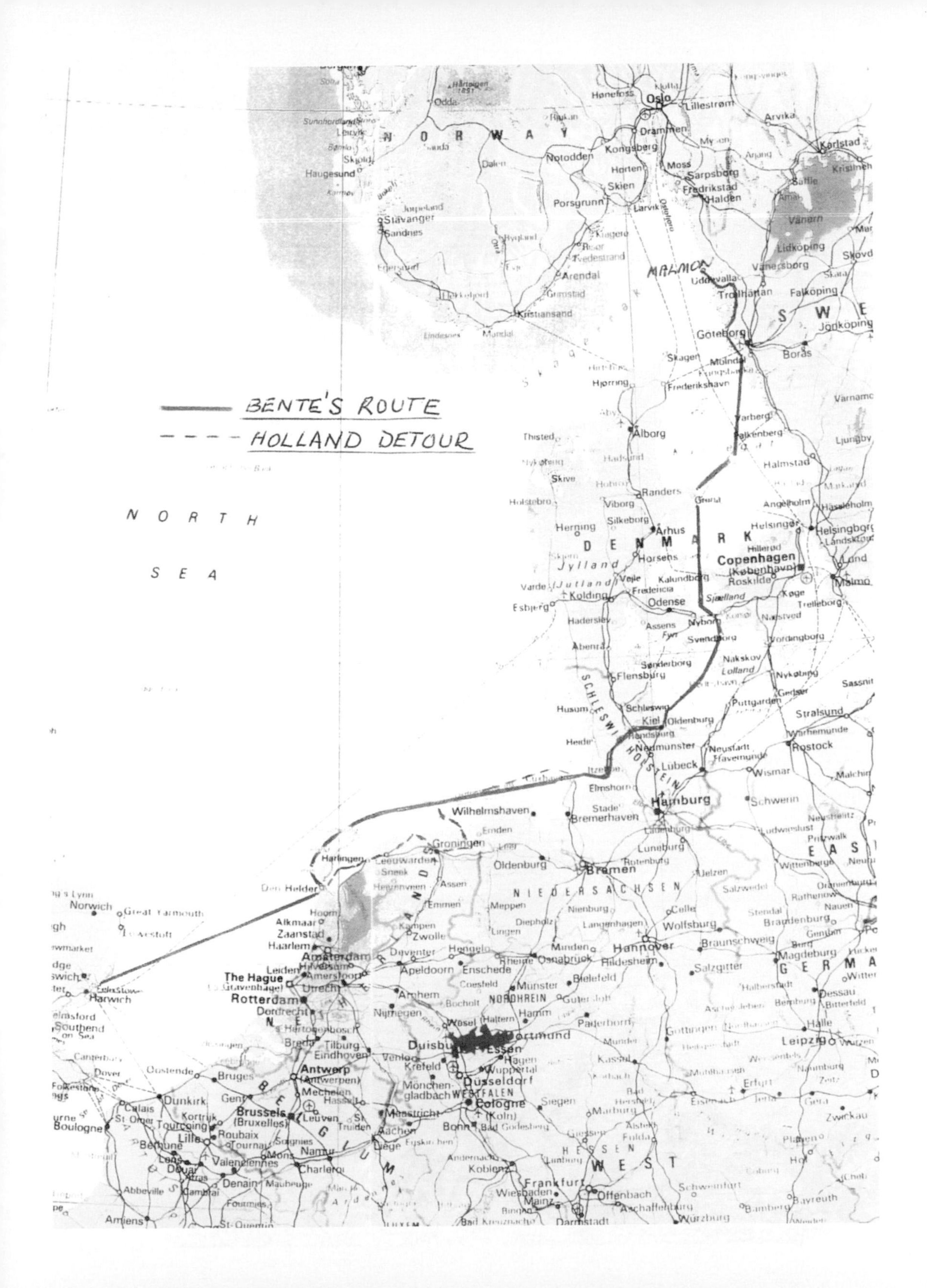
BENTE'S ROUTE
HOLLAND DETOUR
NORTH
SEA
MALMON
NORWAY
DENMARK
Oslo
Drammen
Kongsberg
Notodden
Moss
Sarpsborg
Fredrikstad
Halden
Horten
Skien
Porsgrunn
Larvik
Stavanger
Sandnes
Haugesund
Arendal
Kristiansand
Uddevalla
Trollhättan
Göteborg
Frederikshavn
Hjørring
Ålborg
Randers
Århus
Horsens
Copenhagen
(København)
Roskilde
Odense
Nyborg
Svendborg
Kolding
Esbjerg
Flensburg
Schleswig
Kiel
Neumünster
Lübeck
Hamburg
SCHLESWIG HOLSTEIN
Wilhelmshaven
Bremerhaven
Bremen
Groningen
Leeuwarden
Harlingen
Den Helder
Oldenburg
NIEDERSACHSEN
Hannover
Amsterdam
The Hague
Rotterdam
Utrecht
Harwich
Norwich
Antwerp
Brussels
BELGIUM
Duisburg
Essen
Düsseldorf
Cologne
Dortmund
Frankfurt
Halmstad
Helsingborg
Malmö
Rostock
Leipzig
Magdeburg

TO CUXHAVEN
To Cuxhaven
EAST FRISIAN ISLANDS
WEST FRISIAN ISLANDS
NORTH SEA
NETHERLANDS
Cuxhaven
Wilhelmshaven
Emden
Groningen
Harlingen
Den Helder
Alkmaar
Haarlem
Amsterdam
Katwijk ann Zee
Leiden
's Gravenhage (The Hague)
Zoetermeer
Utrecht
Rotterdam
Dordrecht
Arnhem
Nijmegen
Breda
Tilburg
Eindhoven
Apeldoorn
Zwolle
Deventer
Enschede
Münster
Osnabrück
Bielefeld
Dortmund
Essen
Duisburg
Düsseldorf
Krefeld
Mönchengladbach
Köln
Aachen
Maastricht
Antwerpen
Brugge
Gent
Calais
Boulogne -sur-Mer
Great Yarmouth
Lowestoft
Ipswich
Felixstowe
Harwich
Clacton on Sea
Margate
Ramsgate
Dover
Vlissingen (Flushing)
Middelburg
NORTH
SEA
TERSCHELLING
AMELAND
VLIELAND
TEXEL
Harlingen
FRIESLAND
GRONINGEN
DRENTHE
OVERIJSSEL
GELDERLAND
NOORD HOLLAND
AMSTERDAM
HAARLEM
IJSSELMEER (ZUIDER ZEE)
Markerwaard (West Polder)
Oost Flevoland
Zuid Flevoland
Noord Oost Polder
Enkhuizen
Alkmaar
Den Helder
Hilversum
Apeldoorn
Deventer
Hengelo
Meppel
'S GRAVENHAGE (THE HAGUE)
Scheveningen
Delft
ZUID HOLLAND
ROTTERDAM
Hoek van Holland
UTRECHT
NIJMEGEN
Dordrecht
Schouwen
Walcheren
ZEELAND
Vlissingen (Flushing)
Breda
TILBURG
NOORD BRABANT
Hertogenbosch
EINDHOVEN
ANTWERPEN
KREFELD
DUSSELDORF
BRUGGE
Zeebrugge

Deck Shots

Cabin Interior

Sailing alone
near the
Isle of Wight

Flying *the* flag

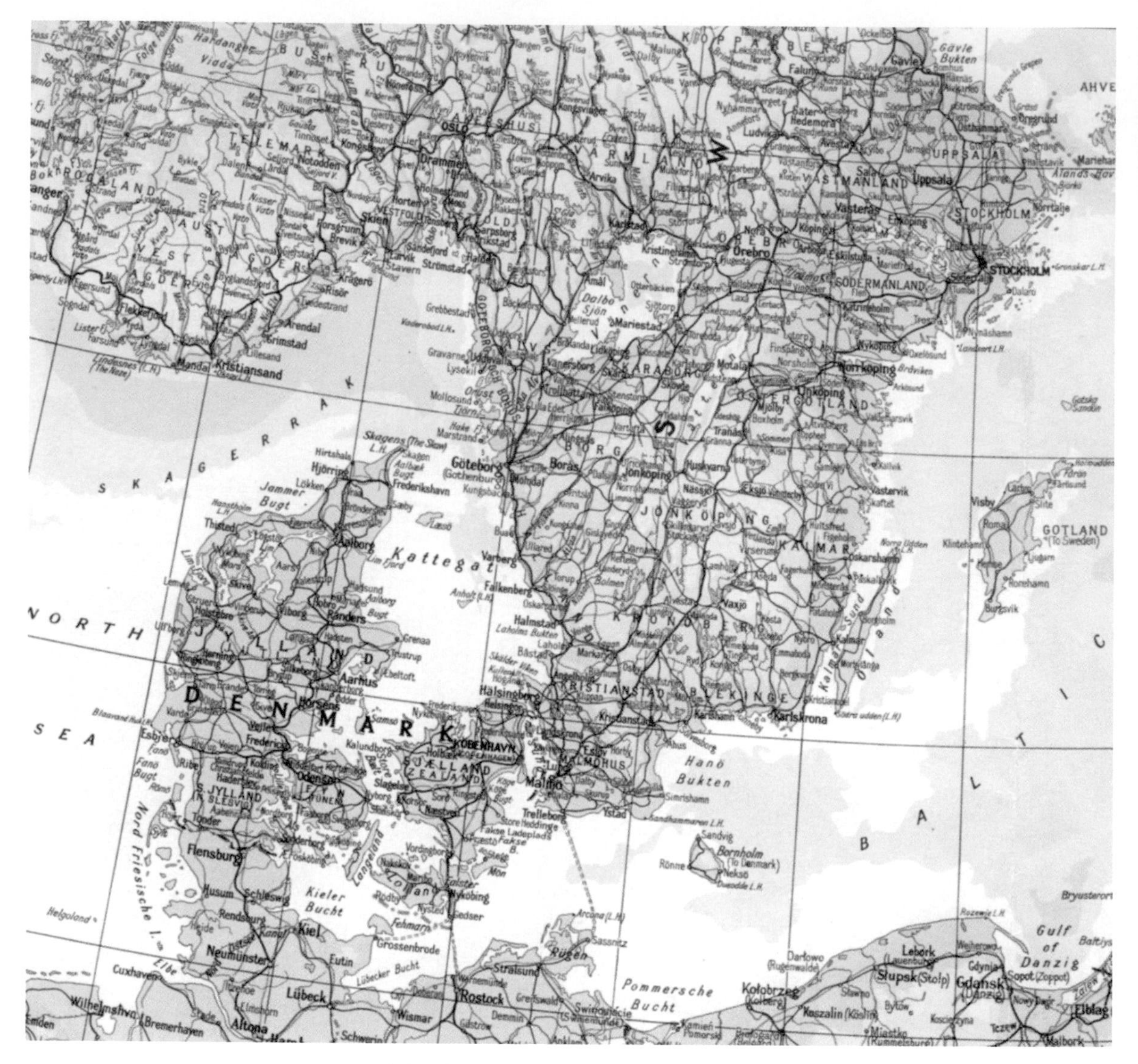

Trip (June 26 - August 25, 1993)

The start … *Bente* leaving moorings at Waldringfield. June 26th

A Kiel Canal view… "a little closer, please!"

A doddle through the Kiel Canal

Safe arrival to Bohus Malmon … the party starts

Ian always flew the Canadian flag

The skipper … starting back from Bohus Malmon

… with Gunne at the helm…

Telling how it was! … L to R, Eva-Lena, Oili, George, Ian

Ian

There are few things in this world that produce a greater sense of satisfaction than to sail your own boat across the sea and into a foreign port.

Hammond Innes

The excitement of Christmas and New Year's had subsided into the dark cold days of January, and my thoughts wandered to warmer climes with imaginings of sun speckled seas, gentle breezes, and the magic of sailing.

It was shortly after my usual visit to the annual boat show at Earls Court that I was sitting at home daydreaming, and my wife, sensing my mood asked, "What are your plans for sailing *Bente* next summer? You will have to *do something* after all the work you have been doing on her.

"Why don't you sail up to Sweden and spend some time with Papa Gunne? He would love it.

"I expect I will drive up again this summer so we could be together part of the time."

Well, that was a bit of a challenge!

I wondered.

Why not? Certainly dear old *Bente* would be ready, despite her advancing years, after the complete refit I had given her over the past two years.

It *would* be lovely to sail again in those waters on the west coast of Sweden, with its thousands of rocky islands, little coves, and beaches, giving an infinite variety of passages and havens. And the clear tideless waters warmed by the Gulf Stream. The long sunny days of the Swedish summer, with fresh sea food, bonfires on beaches, and the many family and friends up there.

What a tempting idea.

Bente, built in Skjeberg, Norway, just north of this Swedish west coast vacationland, is ideal for these waters and her type was in fact known as a 'skerries cruiser'. With a long overhanging bow and swept back keel she is excellent for nosing onto those rocky shores, with a stern anchor out in the local way, and I had designed her new pulpit open forward for ease of stepping ashore.

Of course, I *had* sailed *Bente* from Portsmouth up to Sweden back in '84, her first voyage after being rebuilt, but it was a rushed trip using a delivery skipper, so I was really crew, and we had gone non-stop so didn't see all that much. Just enough to want to come back one day and do it in a more leisurely fashion. Thereafter there were three lovely summers cruising the west coast of Sweden, and up into the Oslo fjord of Norway, before crossing Sweden via the Gota Canal to the Baltic side.

So I had a rough idea of how to get up there, and quite good knowledge of the coast of Sweden north of Gothenburg.

There were many positive aspects to such a trip, but what about drawbacks or problems?

Well, there is that long, exposed North Sea crossing to make before getting into the more sheltered waters of the South West Baltic. That would need some careful planning and a bit of luck with the weather.

It would be no fun to be caught out in a gale with the sand shallows of the Frisian Islands to leeward reaching out at you. The sands are littered with the wrecks of those who ventured too close! There are now some harbours among the islands, accessible to sailing yachts, and providing shelter if not much else in the way of facilities, but the approaches to most of them are a bit daunting to strangers. Twisting channels, dangerous shallows each side, and fast flowing tidal streams.

Great care would be necessary.

And then I thought, what shall I do about crew?

The family don't sail, and single-handing is out of the question, there being at least two overnight passages in active shipping areas. Maybe my friend George could be persuaded to come if I handle it right. Mind you, he is 70 now so I would have to take care. Like keeping night passages to a minimum. But his Christmas card did ask, 'Are you going cruising in *Bente* next summer?'

He knows the boat well, having come back with me from Copenhagen in 1990. And he certainly is very capable after those many years working and sailing in the tough conditions around Australia. I really don't mind the laconic style he must have acquired out there – he is a bit like an 'over the hill' Crocodile Dundee!

There really ought to be a third crew for comfortable watch keeping at night, but arrangements become increasingly complicated as numbers increase, and the two of us could manage if we had to, I thought.

Out came the charts, the pilot books, (neither very complete or up to date for Danish and Swedish waters), the new *Reeds Nautical Almanac,* tidal stream data, and all other possible references, and I spent many pleasant hours lost in planning and replanning each leg of the yet 'maybe' trip.

I dropped in on George and his wife Beryl in Ramsey on my way back from a day at the Beaulieu boat jumble in early April. Over tea and cakes, I hinted that I was toying with the idea of sailing up to Sweden in the summer. I carefully avoided being too specific, or suggesting that he come as crew. That would be for later!

George mentioned, significantly, that he was working in a local DIY shop three days a week, but that he could get as much time off as he wanted. He *was* interested!

Spring came, and with it the varnishing of the brightwork, antifouling, ferrying mountains of gear back on board from winter storage at my home in Surrey, to the boatyard in Suffolk, then launching and rigging, and the hundreds of little jobs to make everything ready for another season.

Then George accepted an invitation to spend a leisurely early June weekend pottering about on the river Deben. On arrival late Saturday afternoon we by chance met Kristiane and Julian who insisted we join them for a small sail down the river, and to share their dinner on board *Trinike*, their Rival 32.

We were just threading our way through the fleet of moored boats at Ramsholt when Julian noticed that Grant and Sheila were on board their boat *Sharon*, so we rafted up and shared a pleasant evening of good food, wine, and company.

We sailed back up to the mooring at Waldringfield in moonlight. Sometime in the evening I asked George if he thought we should "have a go" at cruising up to Sweden. He took the bait and that was that!

'Kick off' was set for Saturday June 26th. This would take advantage of the long days of light, even if we would miss the actual midsummer celebrations in Sweden, and we would have 2-3 weeks up there before having to start back in early August to avoid the increasingly hostile weather that invades the Skaggerak as August progresses.

The remaining days of June were for me a blur of all the details of shopping, storing, and checking all necessary for a good safe trip. George would not be available until the morning of the 26th so it was basically all up to me.

We agreed that departure, and indeed each leg of the trip, would depend upon a reasonable weather outlook, so as the day of departure approached I watched the Atlantic weather patterns in the morning paper, and contacted the Met Office on the 25th.

Their 3 and 5 day forecasts (faxed to our local copy shop) showed a high (1030) southwest of Lands End, and a moderate low (994) south of Iceland. Both were expected to move northeastward so the high was expected to dominate conditions in the Southern North Sea areas from Saturday through Monday at least.

The detail for our crossing area was – Saturday afternoon Westerly force 3-4 occasionally 5, becoming Northwesterly 3-4 at night. Perfect! Mostly cloudy with some light rain at first, but that wouldn't matter. Sunday was forecast Northwesterly 4-5, becoming dry with broken cloud.

With luck, we would have conditions for a brisk crossing with the wind abaft the port beam. The forecast risk of sea mist or fog patches was noted but didn't seem to fit the rest of the conditions so wasn't taken very seriously.

The first leg would be across to Den Helder on the Dutch coast. This was just at the beginning of the route up the Frisian Islands. We could nip in there for overnight with hardly any detour from our route. It was the Dutch navy base and had a yacht club, so it should be ideal for an overnight rest on Sunday night after the 140 mile crossing, and before the next big leg of 170 miles or so up to the River Elbe and the Kiel Canal into the Baltic.

Once into the Elbe River we would have generally sheltered waters through the Kiel Canal, then the Danish Islands, an open leg across the Kattegat to Gothenberg, and finally up the inside passage through the beautiful islands up the Swedish coast to Bohus Malmon.

All of our route planning was to be based on an average speed of five knots and we would use the engine as necessary to achieve that. Thus we had to allow 28 hours for the crossing to Den Helder.

Very conveniently there was a high water Harwich at about 1600 hours on Saturday the 26th, so we could use the ebb stream to start us on our way, cross the coastal shipping lanes before dark, and not reach the main deep water north-south shipping lanes until after daybreak.

The short hours of darkness are a real help! We should reach port in 28 hours, say by 2000 hours latest, still in daylight, but earlier if we get a good breeze with which *Bente* can make six to seven knots.

day 1 ✧ Saturday June 26th

Suddenly it was our day of departure! We dropped the customs form off at their office in Felixstowe Docks, en route to Waldringfield, and then after putting the last of the provisions on board, and lashing the Metzler dinghy on the foredeck, we were all ready.

My wife, Oili, and son Alan, waved and photographed from the boatyard as we started motoring downriver towards the sea. The breeze was astern but too light to enable us to make way against the last of the flood. It was just two o'clock so we had plenty of time to cover the six miles to the sea by high water.

The feeling of excitement was difficult to suppress so I busied myself in preparing the sails, and a last check of rigging and lashings, and George took the helm with just traces of a smile twitching the corners of his mouth. Grant and Sheila waved vigorously from the cockpit of *Sharon* as we passed them at Ramsbolt.

The Deben bar, so formidable to strangers, and requiring a new chart each spring to show the shifts of its sand after the winter storms, slipped beneath our keel at 1610 hours and we were away. I had programmed the Texel light vessel on co-ordinates into the Decca navigator as our first waypoint, and our course to make good was 070 degrees.

Conditions out at sea were good with a westerly breeze of force 3, and hardly any sea running, but it was hot and humid with low cloud cover, so the warm front had just passed and should be followed during the night by the cold front, and wind veering northwesterly. The high pressure system would begin to take over during Sunday.

We made sail and I took the opportunity to try out the new jib I had acquired just the week before to give us more headsail options. Its 120 square feet would be a better working sail size than the 230 square foot yankee and should still work well with the 92-square-foot staysail

Hopefully there would be less foredeck sail changing, especially at night. Total sail area with this one set would be just under 400 square feet, but *Bente* was designed to the 40-square-metre (400 sq. ft.) racing rule (so popular in Europe in the 20's and 30's) so that should be just right.

We streamed the Wasp log, even though the Decca Navstar gave us more accurate speed over ground information, and it showed us churning through the water at a reassuring 5 to 6 knots.

Watchkeeping at night, in these conditions, was decided on a three hour rota which would mean no deep sleep, but no exhaustion at the helm either, and we could catch up on sleep Sunday night in Den Helder. George wanted us to steer using the Autohelm, but I was concerned about battery drain so I insisted,

'Come on, George, you have to steer to enjoy sailing!'

I needn't have been so cautious really, for besides the two new 75 amp hour Tudor batteries in parallel for the main system, I had bought another and stowed it as a spare to use for engine starting if the need should ever arise. It never did!

George opted to take the midnight to three a.m. watch, which would be the only fully dark one, as the sky would not be really dark until well after 10 p.m. at this time of year, and it would start to lighten up again soon after 3 a.m.

It was a peaceful night and morning, with no ships anywhere near to disturb our communion with nature. The Sestrel Moore compass is mounted so that it is in line with the horizon forward when sitting at the helm, so keeping course couldn't be easier. And of course with her long keel and well balanced ends *Bente* almost steers herself and needs only the occasional light touch on the helm.

In the early afternoon we were approached by a small trawler performing guardship duties for a ship doing a seismic sounding survey and dragging a line two miles astern. Being absorbed in our own little world we had not paid any attention to the CH. 16 broadcasts about their activities and position until the guard ship came close and suddenly called us by name, "*Bente,* please alter your course to south and detour around the trailing guardship!"

We quickly fell over ourselves to comply. They had the courtesy to call later and say,

'O.K. *Bente,* resume your course and thank you.'

We were mystified by being unable to see the Texel lightship when by midafternoon we should have been right on top of its way point position.

Was the Navstar misbehaving? Other marks had been right where we expected! There was a large catamaran type structure, with what looked like a helicopter landing platform a few miles west of us, but not marked on our chart. All very confusing! We just put it down to a Decca error and moved on to our next waypoint – the red/white buoy marking the start of the long channel into the Waddensee from the southwest. Den Helder was just inside.

It was over drinks in the yacht club later that evening that we learned that the unthinkable had happened – the Dutch authorities had dispensed with this famous old lightship mark, with its powerful beacon, which had guided sailors over long distances for many years. Apparently modern navigation methods made it redundant. What we had seen to the west was a new gas well platform. So much for using an old chart!

The rest of the approach to Den Helder was routine, but under engine, as our course became more northerly and the wind had by now veered into the northwest. It was rather a slog against the still ebbing tide, but there was no point waiting until it turned sometime after seven o'clock – we would be safely in by then.

I called up the Port Control on channel 12 as recommended in the almanac, this being the main Dutch navy base, and we were given a warm welcome. We were close enough that they may have seen the Canadian ensign we fly.

The yacht club harbour, close by the entrance, is small but well organized and staffed, and we were very politely and efficiently guided to secure alongside another English sloop. They had just arrived from River Orwell after starting out on Saturday morning! They would have been against the tide until late afternoon so we did well to wait. This Westerly Longbow with a crew of 5 were outbound up the Frisians to Borkum. Good to know that Borkum is a good enough harbour to be a cruising destination.

The bar cum restaurant on the upper level of the small floating clubhouse had simple but good food, especially if you like Indonesian with a fried egg on top, whatever you order, and was very popular with its Dutch Navy members and their grateful visitors. Good humour abounded.

Fuel was available but not before 9 a.m. nor after 6 p.m. Not too helpful to transit boats like ourselves. Weather charts and information were posted daily – not surprising for a Navy Base.

The B.B.C. forecast 1750 hours had offered winds of northwest force 7 for the German Bight for tomorrow, Monday, but in the pub we were assured that the local forecast gave a more hopeful view of winds moderating to force 3/4 in the morning.

It did blow in the night, but being tired and with full stomachs we slept soundly.

day 3 ✧ Monday June 28th

Up for the B.B.C. 4 radio forecast at 0555 (locally 655) which agreed with the Dutch and gave a comfortable NW 3/4 becoming variable for the German Bight – so the high predicted in the long range forecast was catching us up and with any luck would proceed northeast with us. Excellent!

We set off immediately so as to catch the last hours of the ebb out of the Molengat channel northwestward from the Waddensee back to the North Sea off Texel Island.

Our options for the next stop were either the island of Helgoland, 150 miles away, Cuxhaven, 170 miles away in the Elbe River, or if possible the small marina just inside the entrance lock of the Kiel Canal at Brunsbuttel, another 20 miles further on.

The Elbe light vessel, marking the entrance to the channel up this busy river was also 150 miles away, abeam of Helgoland. Thus we needed 30 hours to reach the light vessel (or a safe haven in Helgoland if required) and we should be there by 1400 hours on Tuesday, just in time to catch the start of the flood tide up the Elbe.

We would need all of the six plus hours of flood to cover the nearly 40 miles up to the lock at Brunsbuttel.

If we are late we can overnight at Cuxhaven, but that was not very convenient, because we would miss a day waiting for a flood tide so we could finish the trip up the Elbe. The tidal stream in the river flows at over 3 knots and I didn't fancy struggling against that with our 5 knot cruising speed!

Motoring out the Molengat channel we battled a nasty chop caused by the headwind over ebbing tide, but that was nothing compared to the mad gyrations we suffered when the fishing fleet of trawlers charged past us at full speed to get out to their fishing grounds off Texel. They went past, one after the other, maybe eight of them, to prolong the agony. Occasionally a face peered at us from a bridge with a look of complete disinterest, as if they couldn't hear my muttered oaths!

Once clear we hoisted sail but kept the engine going to help us tack out to get good sea room to weather off Texel and its long sand banks.

Finally we were able to turn north, close hauled, to parallel the shore of the island at a safe distance. The breaking surf off our lee bow was a stark reminder. By midday the wind had dropped to the point where we were below our target speed of 5 knots, so it was "on engine". At 1615 we were opposite the western end of Amieland, so we were comfortably on schedule with 100 miles to go in 22 hours.

Later we moved further offshore to pick up the line of green starboard hand flashing buoys marking the edge of the main ship channel, and separating it from the inshore shipping zone. They are spaced about 6 miles apart and we would use them, from just outside the channel, as "stepping stones" for night navigation all the way to the Elbe. Almost as soon as one flashing light is passed the next can be faintly detected.

The Navstar had refused to start when we left Ben Helder, and I had decided it would be easier to sort out in the Kiel Canal. Until then we would be navigating in the old fashioned way, and these flashing buoys would be very handy!

Motorsailing along just before sunset about 50 yards outside the buoys, George had just gone below leaving me on watch, when a voice, quite loud, from the V.H.P. (which we leave always listening on Ch. 16 said,

"Sailboat, I am right behind you!"

That certainly woke me from my reverie and on my feet in a flash!

There it was, a small very neat oil coaster, astern but safely off our port quarter. Once I responded to him on the V.H.F. he explained in a clearly German accent that I should be much further inshore – out of what he considered to be "his" territory, obviously. I thanked him for his helpful advice, and we carried on our quite legitimate course.

day 4 ✧ Tuesday June 29th

The wind eased further during the night and by daybreak was too little to use, and it was becoming northeasterly, so we motored with headsails down and main flattened.

The sea was as flat as a millpond and there was just enough sea mist to make us wonder if we might face some visibility problems. However, the green buoys had appeared like clockwork. So far so good. At 0900 we identified the last of them and carried on the same course for the Elbe Light Vessel. By 1200 it should have been in sight but wasn't.

There was Helgoland in the distance just abaft our port beam, where it should be, and quite a variety of marks off to starboard, with one in particular tall red one which we thought might mark the passage into the river Weser. But no lightship ahead of us where it ought to be. Surely they couldn't have taken away the Elbe L.V. like the Texel. *No!* This chart is this year's!

There was only one thing to do – motor over to the red mark and identify it. Couldn't really tell its size, therefore how far away it was, but maybe 4 or 5 miles. That shouldn't take long. We might still make our schedule. Well it seemed to take forever, but gradually we could see that it was quite tall, and the almanac gave the height of the Elbe L.V. as12 metres, so maybe?

Soon we could see it was an L.V., and then we were alongside and saw *ELBE 1*. It was moored bow on to the prevailing westerly winds and in line with its narrow boom, it looked just like a buoy. We had clearly been pushed quite a lot to the north of our track by the flow of ebb tide coming out of the river Weser way to the south of us. More care should have been taken with plotting our dead reckoning position!

By now it was 13.30. We had half an hour in hand before low water Cuxhaven, and eventual change in tidal stream to flooding up the Elbe. There had been just the last traces of ebb flowing past the L.V. which confirmed an imminent change. Great! We were on schedule and had a good chance of making it to Brunsbuttel by evening. A breeze appeared from astern, so it was back to full sail.

Before long we were churning along and were able to do without engine. Other sailboats converged on the route from both sides, and soon we were part of a large fleet with reachers, spinnakers, (our yankee) plus a strengthening flood tide pushing us along at increasing speed.

There was inevitably a bit of racing and jockeying for position among us to liven things up a little. Soon we had full flood and were speeding past channel markers that were leaning from the tide with a large bow wave and long swirling wakes downstream. Cuxhaven slipped by and we began to lose some of our companions as they turned into various havens along the river.

Dodging ferries, container ships, tankers, Navy gunboats and what have you, we crossed over the channel to the port side and sailed up the inside of the long bend to port toward Brunsbuttel, which we could now see identified by its tall radio tower. The lock was open and nearly full as we arrived. We had covered the 40 miles in just a shade over 5 hours. That was some going!

Soon the lock was chock-a-block and we were through and turning to port, with almost everyone else, into the handy little marina. This marina is apparently nearly always full in season, and some people use it like a summer camp, but we managed to squeeze in.

We weren't to be stopped after the long trip we had just made!

Probably we weren't as tired as we were in need of a good feed. Neither George nor I are much good at preparing meals at sea, so we exist on cup-a-soup, sandwiches, and lots of cakes, especially frangipanes. Our reward for completing a leg is to go ashore for a big meal!

There were excellent shower facilities ashore, and then we were off up the street, stopping only to phone home before diving into a good looking little Italian restaurant, to stuff ourselves with a mountainous salad plate and repeating bottles of German beer. A well deserved feast, we thought!

day 5 ✧ Wednesday June 30th

The Kiel Canal is 98 kilometres from lock to lock, which meant about 11 hours at our cruising speed of 5 knots. We wanted to clear the northern lock at Holtenau, the Baltic end, and go up another 8 miles or so to the Kiel Yacht Club at Strande, where we had been so well treated in 1990. Our cutlass bearing had failed on the way there from Langeland, and we had sailed into harbour. It was also handy to a supermarket, a last chance to stock up on German beer, bread, and whatever other goodies. There was also, I remembered, a very convenient fuel dock, and I had estimated that we would by then surely be in need of a refill.

It had to be another early start, and we were away by 0730 enjoying a leisurely breakfast as we motored along. It was overcast at first but cleared slowly and gave us a very pleasant, relaxed day.

You are allowed to motorsail on the canal (not sail only) but there wasn't enough breeze to make it worthwhile. The weather conditions, with the overcast and light winds from a generally northerly sector, suggested that the centre of the high pressure area was just west of us, and we should have calm conditions for at least the next day or two.

After breakfast I took out my little circuit tester and set about to find the trouble with the Navstar. It wasn't long until I traced it to the fused switchbox and found a bit of oxidation on its fuse contact, and had it back in operation straightaway.

The scenery was mostly pastoral with few people but many animals gazing at us as we passed by with our tiny wake rippling along the banks. There were occasional ducks and swans, the odd string of cyclists on the towpath, and small groups of children shrieking at play by the water edge.

The only navigational activity was to be sure to dodge the little ferries that dart from one road and to the other, sometimes right on our bows, and to almost hold our breath as we squeezed past some monster container ship that seemed to fill the whole width of the canal. To make it even more interesting, George dug out his camera and had me steer up under the bows of one so he could make an impressive photo. Hopefully its captain couldn't see us or he might have blown a fuse! We passed some magnificent racing yachts in the maxi category, which may have been on their way home after competing in the Kiel Week races.

The huge light towers along the way used to control traffic had regularly shown green, but then suddenly we had three flashing reds meaning all vessels stop!

We secured to one of the wooden pilings on the edge of the canal for a half hour, and were greened on our way again. Up ahead we found a dredging operation which had caused the stop as they replaced the receiving barge. There was a widening operation under way on a typically massive German scale.

One last bend and there was the Holtenau lock. It was just 1900. There was traffic congestion here but we were through after an hour. Fee paying is now centred here and is based on length – our fee for 10.5 metres was 31 DM. We motored up the Kieler Bucht through hordes of traffic both commercial and pleasure. There are many yacht clubs (or marinas) on each side.

Shortly after 2100 we were moored in the Kiel Yacht Club – alongside the fuelling barge which was the only free place we could find that late. At least it would be handy in the morning! It was a pleasant evening with a bright sunset so we dined in the cockpit using for the first time the new table I had built at home last winter. After some soup, scrambled eggs, wine, cheese and biscuits, coffee with liqueurs, and a Barbara Streisand concert, we crashed.

day 6 ✧ Thursday July 1st

The local supermarket was open conveniently at 0730, so we bought fresh bread, milk, German beer, and a few impulse items for the ever-present sweet tooth! The fuel station came to life at 0800 and we filled 77.5 litres which meant we had been down to 12.5 litres.

We were now out of range of B.B.C. longwave radio weather forecasts and would have to rely on harbourmasters' information at each stop until we reached Swedish broadcast areas. They give gale warnings in English and I could understand enough Swedish to get the gist of their daily regional forecasts.

At the Kiel Y.C. there was no information posted and no sign of the harbourmaster anywhere, but it was a gorgeous, bright, sunny morning so off we went. There wasn't a breath of wind so we set up the Autohelm on a course for the southern tip of Langeland, 25 miles away, and enjoyed a leisurely breakfast of fresh brodchens with cheese, marmalade, and coffee as our reliable two-cylinder Kubota motored us along.

Soon after midday we were abeam the southern tip of Langeland, and there was a little breeze from a southerly direction. By 1430 it had become force 2/3 from the southeast so we made sail. George was never very keen on bothering with spinnakers, but I thought it was too good an opportunity to miss, and hoisted the lovely three year old red, white, and blue radial spinnaker, used only once before.

On a course of 030 degrees, we were making between 4 and 5 knots, steering with Autohelm, and hardly ever having to touch the sails. The peace and quiet, after so much motoring during the past few days, was much enjoyed. Some impressive ships went by, including the Kron Prince Harald, which we guessed was a ferry from Travemunde to Oslo.

We just followed the shoreline of Langeland with its varied colours of farmland, the occasional farmhouse, one or two villages, and little else. We had yet to decide where we would stop for the night, which was to have depended on how far we progressed. Clearly we wouldn't get far beyond the northern tip in daylight, and decided to make for the island of Omo, some 5 or 6 miles east of there which the pilot book said had a nice harbour.

The chart we were using showed the island but not the harbour location nor any safe approach through the long shallows surrounding it, so we had to 'feel' our way.

Starting from the southwest corner well offshore, we sailed up the west side looking for signs of life on this very bare, but green little island. Finally on the northwest corner there was the telltale cluster of masts sticking up from inside the land. There were no marks of any kind and without a channel there was no way we could get to the island without going around. There was a large sailboat going in a likely direction so we followed it for some way, but then they altered course to go down the east side of the island.

Suddenly a ferry boat came charging into sight and headed right into Omo harbour, so we carved its route into memory, and from 1/2 mile or so astern of it tried to follow the course it had taken. Using the Hecta echo sounder always makes me nervous, so I prefer not to, but on this occasion we certainly did, and found our way forward tenderly along a channel of about 9-feet depth.

Eventually we were rewarded by what George described, writing later in the log in an unusual burst of exclamation, as a "lovely little harbour" and "sweet little island." We had made a useful 60 miles.

The main harbour of marina-type berths seemed full of Danish and German flags, (and hanging laundry suggesting semi-permanent residence) but there was just room for us on the main dock (visitors' quay) to starboard, leading into the ferry boat landing, and the little fishing boat harbour. We secured just ahead of an ageing Baltic trader. There were obviously no restaurants nearby so we dined aboard and later went exploring ashore.

It seemed to be little more than a summer holiday island, with no town or village or even church to be seen, but it surely was beautiful and peaceful. The harbour area had one building comprising a fishing storehouse and a sort of community hall, with a separate modern building housing toilets, showers, and laundry, and the inevitable kiosk which provided an after dinner treat of ice cream served by a pretty college student who enjoyed practicing her English for the first time that summer.

There was a road which may have led to some more civilization, and a rumour of a disco somewhere along it, but we decided against attending. Tomorrow would have to be an early start, and a long, fast, day if we were to cover the nearly 100 miles to Anholt, the Danish island in the Kattegat, which was our next port of call.

The Baltic trader had a couple of families with children on for what they described as a week's inexpensive cruise. Hopefully they wouldn't go too far because she looked a bit run down, and had some obviously soft wood about her – including the rudder head.

day 7 ✧ Friday July 2nd

The wind rose in the night and gave us that all too familiar scream in the rigging. When we came on deck in the early morning it was blowing force 3/4 from the NNW with a lumpy sea and gloomy skies. Not a very pleasant outlook. Our course would be dead upwind, at least at first.

It would be slow and bouncy going, but it was unlikely to become much stronger, and if we worked toward a more sheltered area upwind like Kerteminde Bay we could decide there whether to carry on or go into Kerteminde for the day.

We cast off at 0500, and retraced from memory the unmarked channel, and then turned north up the main northbound shipping route off Korsor. It was a bit of a slog, but when we reached the first of the channel marks we noticed a tidal stream of about one knot in our favour and that gave us a great boost.

I had read that although the Baltic, and the Kattegat and Skaggerak, have only a few inches of tide range, there are tidal currents accentuated by winds which can be as much as a knot, but they are not as easy to understand or predict, at least for foreigners.

Ahead of us was the procession of ferry ships crossing each way the 15 mile gap between Nyborg to port and Korsor to our starboard, and then we could see the bridge-causeway complex under construction to replace them on this principal traffic route. It was about half complete, with a causeway on stilts from Nyborg to the little island half way.

The eastern section was well under way, with most of the pylon bases for the bridge sections under which ships would pass ahead of us in place. Threading through the stream of ferry ships we cleared the temporary narrow ship channel through the construction area, and at 0700 turned northwesterly toward Kerteminde bay.

Later, a rather rusty small freighter flying the Maltese flag crossed our path heading due south toward the causeway. We wondered, and the more so when we heard a Danish coast radio voice trying to raise the ship by name on CH. 16, again and again.

I hope they had a better lookout than they had radio watch! Maybe they, too, had a 3-year-old Admiralty chart that showed no sign whatever of any causeway project despite its many years in progress.

By 0940 we were up close to the headland on the north side of Kerteminde bay and, as the wind seemed to be backing a little, we decided it was worth trying to sail. The course from here to clear Rosnaes, the western tip of Zealand, was 350 degrees, which might take some tacking, but after that we would be able to ease a little. It soon became clear that it would be impossible to reach Anholt in daylight, so we opted for Grenna now some 55 miles due north.

The wind continued to back and by midday it was westerly, which made life easier, but there were a few holes in it during which we used the engine to maintain speed, and we arrived in Grenna at 2115, an average of just over 5 knots from the point at Kerteminde. The pilot book had not been enthusiastic about facilities there in 1981, and it looked from a distance rather inhospitable with nothing to see but large factory buildings, tall smoke stacks, oil tanks, and big ferry ships in the harbour.

To our delight we found a brand new marina with excellent shore facilities and restaurant. There was only one empty berth that we could see, which was the very common bow to pontoon with wooden posts for securing the stern. Well, the posts proved to be only 8 feet apart compared to our 8 ft., 6 in. beam, but with much push and shove we squeezed through – much to the delight of a watching crew who "in their cups" found our act "the best of the day."

When we had time to look around we found ourselves in the midst of many lovely classic wooden boats stopping over en route to a festival further north at the famous and beautiful Li fjord.

Exploring ashore we found the harbourmaster's office and a weather forecast of winds 8-13 metres/second (16–25 knots), plus rain, for the next day. There would be an update posted in the morning. It was time to do some forward planning.

The distance to Gothenberg was about 90 miles, which would take optimum conditions to do in a day. It would have been only about 60 odd miles from Anholt, but here we were in Grenna! There were no alternative havens beyond Anholt or Laeso, en route through the Kattegat.

A charming lady skipper of an adjacent beamy, prewar classic was very helpful with information about the approaches to their harbours, so we felt more confident about tomorrow, if not very keen on threading our way through the long shallows surrounding Laeso without detailed charts.

The western approach to Anholt was easy by comparison, so perhaps that is why, of the two islands, Anholt is the more popular among the sailing fraternity.

day 8 ✧ Saturday July 3rd

We woke to rain and the predicted fresh southwesterly. We took our time over breakfast, then checked the harbourmaster's new forecast, which suggested that the rain would stop later. George wisely thought we should make the short trip across to Anholt which would leave us a more manageable leg to Gothenberg the next day.

Underway by 0900, we motorsailed with just the staysail and single-reefed main, and tacked downwind for comfort in the heavy seas which we found as we moved offshore. The distance was only 27 miles so just after midday we could see the island sticking up higher than expected on the horizon in this country of shallow water and sand dunes. The wind and seas were still quite heavy, but they were from astern so no problem.

As we came near, using a compass bearing on the lighthouse to keep us in safe water, we could see a solid ring of sand beach, backed by sand bluffs with grassy hummocks, but behind that was a high hill with a topping of windswept pines. No civilization was seen except on the western tip with its lighthouse, wind generator and the harbour with stone breakwater and a few low buildings.

The harbour was fairly large, but was very full. Few were sailing today, and as usual no one offered us any help or advice on finding a berth. It seems standard practice in Germany and Scandinavia to ignore newcomers.

There was one place with room for us to berth alongside on the windward side of the jetty, which could present problems getting away, but we took it happily, and approached it noisily and aggressively enough to persuade the skipper of a little Dragon-type sailboat to move a couple of metres aft so we could squeeze in ahead of him.

A few people came to chat us up. I suppose the sight of little *Bente* coming into harbour in that wind, flying the Canadian ensign, aroused some curiosity. One said that we were the "darling of the fleet" which warmed us after our wet and bumpy ride.

To our delight we found an excellent supermarket, 2 restaurants, a fuel station, and of course, the inevitable fishing dock and facilities, a kiosk, plus a massive shower and toilet building. For the summer at least, it is a holiday island for campers and day trippers, who arrive from wherever, with their rucksacks and bicycles, on the little ferry boat.

There was a small village inland, away from the sea wind, which George went to see later, in quest of some solitude, I think.

The harbour restaurant had a magnificent grill right in the dining room, in full view, on which they were doing gorgeous steaks. Our choice of fresh salmon was served up with new potatoes, salad, and super Danish beer, all presented by pretty blond girls – all rather splendid, yet dinner cost only $25 for the two of us.

I made a point of telling our waitress that the meal was beautiful, and in prettily accented English she said, "So are you!"

Well!

Back to reality, and on the way back to the boat later we checked the forecast at the H.M. office which was for continuing 8-13 m/s through tomorrow. On today's experience that would mean mostly 13 m/s and above.

We decided to review in the morning.

day 9 ✧ Sunday July 4th

George must have spent a wakeful night because on rising he said he had sensed the wind easing a little toward morning. I didn't argue. It was timely to accept his point of view, so off we would go!

A long line was taken upwind to the breakwater and a bight put over a bollard. After stowing the dinghy back on the foredeck we hauled our bow through the wind, slipped the line, and were away.

Once clear of the harbour breakwater we set full main with staysail, and headed due north for Gothenberg with the wind on our beam. A little later the wind eased so we hoisted the yankee and had a great sail. About midday the wind started to freshen and I began to wonder if the yankee should come down when George poked his head up the companionway and announced in a tone which for him was quite excited,

'I've just heard a gale warning on the V.H.F. – but not where or when!'

I knew it had to be Gothenberg radio, probably through one of its satellite transmitters such as Varberg, 20 miles to leeward, giving a warning as soon as received from their met office. After a brief *tête-à-tête,* George took the helm and I went forward in the agreed routine, reducing sail to double-reefed main and staysail, with the yankee securely lashed to the lee guardrails.

And soon it blew!

We were then still almost 40 miles from Gothenberg – probably 6 hours from the shelter of the islands of the Gothenberg approaches. I had previously traveled the coast to leeward of us, south of Gothenberg, and there weren't any appealing havens there so we decided to carry on as we were.

Bente handled it beautifully and took no water despite her low freeboard – save for a few splashes from crests breaking on her beam and quarter. I was again pleased that I had rigged her old spray dodgers for the first time for this trip.

We eased off 20 to 30 degrees in the puffs and then back up again in the lulls. The Navstar gave us our course to steer, speed over the ground, and the distance to our waypoint which was the Trubaduren lighthouse, and we were much reassured by our excellent progress. Our speed was nearer 7 than 6 knots whenever I checked. The Wasp log was surging mostly out of control.

We soon learned not to worry when the Navstar lost its signals in the deep troughs, and routinely went below to reset it.

By 1400, having studied the chart carefully, we changed our waypoint to the Tistlarna lighthouse, which marked the southern entrance through some islands to the Gothenberg estuary, an improvement of about 5 miles to shelter, and an easier course of 15 degrees East instead of due North.

George steered almost the whole afternoon, with my blessing, because he handled *Bente* so well in the heavy seas. Before long we could see a more constant speck of white on the horizon ahead of us, and then we could see the waves smashing over the rocks (skerries) ahead and to leeward, which meant we were nearing the islands and shelter.

We came up almost to touching the lighthouse perched upon its spray-covered rock, then eased off down a comfortably wide channel toward larger tree-covered islands. It was 1700 hours as we drew into complete shelter, almost a vacuum, and had to drop sails and resort to motor.

It was a striking contrast to the past hours as we slipped through the calm, enjoying the beautiful rocky island scenery all around us.

Only then did I have time to worry whether the Swedish navy would refuse us passage through the 'restricted area' ahead and command us out to sea with their gunboat, as they did when I tried to pass south through here in 1986.

To our delight we found that their base was empty!

The question was, where shall we stop for the night?

There were forests of masts to leeward at Fiskeback, but the access was complicated, especially without detailed local charts, so I decided we would carry on to the island town of Ockero on the north side of the estuary, at the start of the sheltered passage up the coast. By 1800 we emerged out of sheltered waters into the estuary, having almost forgotten the gale 9 or near gale 10 blowing. It hit us with middling fury, and as we turned into it northwestward the spray knifed over and around our hood.

The estuary was like a lake, about a mile wide and open about 3-4 miles upwind to some islands before the open sea. The waves were not as large as out to sea but enough that with windage we could only make about one knot, and the squalls made it touch and go in keeping her head on course.

The engine, a Kubota 17 hp, had plenty of power, but the hull shape meant using a propeller not larger than 13 inches diameter, and I had opted for a two-blade folding type to reduce drag when sailing.

It was a bit worrying to have so little maneuverability in a busy shipping channel, and there were many commercial vessels of all shapes and sizes going to and fro. The spire of the Ockero church stood up on the horizon three miles away to the northwest, beckoning us, so we just slogged away toward it, foot by precious foot. Gradually shelter increased in the lee of the islands, and at 2100 hours we turned into the old 'gasthaven' of Ockero.

What a day that was!

The guest harbour was a disappointment, with the worst facilities we had yet experienced, but we were too tired to care much, and at least it was so unpopular it was almost empty and we had our choice of berths.

After a simple meal we went ashore and phoned my wife's relatives up the coast at Bohus Malmon to report our safe arrival in Sweden, and learned that the forecast for Monday was for gales!

day 10 ✧ Monday July 5th

Gothenberg Radio forecast at 0833 on CH 24 gave gale warnings for all Kattegat, Skaggerak, and Vanern areas, so George and I agreed to take the day off. Much of our route from now on would be in the shelter of islands, but I remembered one stretch between Ockero and Marstrand that was exposed to the sea, and narrow channels among rocks is no place to be in a gale.

Ashore we found an excellent chandlery which had the chart book that I wanted. The whole of the Swedish coast is covered by charts produced for leisure activities in 5 volumes of about 20 charts, at a price of about 350 Kroner (£35).

The harbour was away from the town center, but there was a supermarket and other shops including a library with a tourist information desk, where we obtained information about travel agents for George's flight home, and learned that the nearest customs and immigration offices were in the main ferry terminal in Gothenberg harbour. Fortunately there was a good ferry and connecting bus service to the center so off we went.

George booked himself a flight on Wednesday afternoon, returning July 28th. I would drive him to the airport from Bohus Malmon using my wife's car as long as we were in Malmon, and not still stuck in Ockero!

There was a great tram service from the center downriver to the ferry terminal.

The immigration officer at the ferry terminal was also a yachtsman (so many Swedes are!) just back from cruising in the Stockholm archipelago, so we were well received, and he wrote his name and phone number beside the stamp in my passport in case we ever needed an 'official reference'. He explained that he was rather more than just an immigration officer, more like a British M-16!

The customs people in the next building said they were not interested in us as long as we were not staying more than 3 months, and had nothing to declare. Being suspicious that they just didn't want to bother, I persisted, and was finally able to get a 'reference' from them too.

On the ferry back to Ockero, at about 1830, we noticed that the wind had eased, so we dashed aboard and cast off for Marstrand, a 2 or 3 hour run under power. With luck we would just make it in daylight.

With the new charts and my improving recollection of my previous passage, it should be quite straightforward.

Part of the route was open to the sea but we found that the waves had declined considerably already. Before long a massive fort on the horizon ahead of us identified the famous old town of Marstrand.

Originally a strategic navy base in the conflicts with the Danes, its location and superb deep harbour, surrounded by three islands, with only narrow passages into it, gave complete shelter right next to the open sea, and made it today the premier yacht racing center on the west coast of Sweden.

Our approach was through the southern passage, which at one point was hardly 10 metres wide with steep rock faces to each side. Then suddenly we were through, and there was Marstrand.

To starboard were commercial docks, for navy fishing and larger yachts, and to port the island and town of Marstrand itself. A long stone wharf ran the whole kilometre length of its waterfrontage, and for much of that there were finger jetties sticking out. They were packed chock-a-block with sailing yachts. Most of them were obviously racing machines.

Finding a berth was a problem, and no help was offered. Quite the contrary, when we did find a place alongside a large schooner, we were rebuffed by a young female giving hollow excuses about "expecting a friend." Eventually we went bow on to the main wharf, along to the north end in an area reserved for use by rowing dinghies for hire. I guess some were on hire overnight!

Overlooking the wharf were many lovely old buildings, of perhaps Victorian age architecture, all being lived in and in pristine condition, of timber construction, with ornate carved trim, and all in pastel colours of light grey, pale blue and white. A few shops and restaurants showed the same style and care, so there must have been strict preservation controls on the town.

Sadly, we felt the whole effect was spoiled by the behaviour of the people from the yachts, mostly rowdy and drunken. Quite usual these days, I suppose, for a racing venue, but rather out of character with these elegant surroundings. The restaurants are very expensive if you can even get in! For cruising yachts, Marstrand is worth passing through for a look, but not stopping, at least not in the racing season.

We settled for a simple meal on board, and then made the required phone calls, one to warn relatives that we would make Bohus Malmon by the next evening. The noise of the revelers went on until the early morning.

day 11 ✦ Tuesday July 6th

Away at 0630 under skies of broken cloud, we motored out the north-westerly passage to the open sea into the teeth of a fresh breeze. The seas were yet modest, and soon we were able to ease around to starboard and head down channel toward the route up the inside of the large islands of Tjorn and then Orust. To port was a harbour on the island of Stora Dyron which looked inviting and would make a good alternative to Marstrand on the way back.

By midmorning we reached the bridge at Stenningsund, which fascinated George, and he was busy with his camera. We thought we could lay the channel for a good distance, so we hoisted full sail and managed to carry it all the way to just before the bridge at the gap between Bokenaset on the mainland, and Vindon on the northern tip of Orust. Here is where the Vindo yachts are built.

For the previous hour or two we had been playing tag through a series of wind shadows and gusts with a lovely 9 metre Norwegian sloop called *Sophia*, whose owner took at least one photo of us. I wished I could arrange to get a copy, but she turned away through a short cut too rocky and shallow for my taste, and we did not see her again.

We downed sails to pass under the bridge, proceeded westward in the Havstensfjord with quite a few other sailboats, also under power, and most of them passing us at our leisurely 5 knot cruising speed. Then southwest along the same waterway which becomes the Kalvo and Koljo fjords, until we turned into an almost hidden entrance to the lovely Malostrommar shortcut across the neck of land to the next large fjord at Lysekil.

This was open water again, the wind was quite fresh, and there was a good sea running up the fjord. However, it was now only 6 miles or so to Bohus Malmon, and part of that was in the lee of rocks and islands, so we bashed on.

George went below for a nap and I savoured the last miles of this first leg of a rather challenging adventure.

Rounding a last rock headland, there was the large well-equipped marina at Bohus Malmon, with the well-loved little village behind it.

There was plenty of room, and by 1700 we were secured alongside. A phone call to the Swedish family, and soon there was a party under way on board.

By pure coincidence (I think), within an hour, my wife arrived by car from Norway with the friend she had been visiting, and the party gathered momentum.

Mari, the Norwegian, was the niece of *Bente's* builder, and the town of Skjeberg, where builder Iverson's yard was located, had been their summer home for many years.

Next, Gunnar, Mari's husband, arrived from a convenient business trip in Sweden, and the party went into high gear. Gunnar had crewed with me several times on *Bente's* earlier Scandanavian exploits.

Later we enjoyed, all together, a huge meal put on by Gunne's daughter Eva-Lena at their summer house on the island, and savoured in good company the finality of our arrival.

day 12 ✧ Wednesday July 7th

With Gunne as guide, my wife Oili and I drove George down to Gothenberg center where he could pick up his ticket and the bus to the new airport for his midafternoon flight back to London. Then we took the slow inter-island route back, crisscrossing over islands and bridges along the route *Bente* had traveled just the day before. The scenery was even more majestic than when viewed from the water.

It was a bit faster, too!

✧ days 13 to 33

Then followed three weeks of the worst summer weather I have ever experienced in Sweden.

This has been echoed by every Swede I have talked to since, so it was quite general for the whole country.

Oili left July 12 for a driving holiday visiting family and friends in Sweden and Finland, so I was on my own on board.

I can remember only three days when it wasn't pouring with rain and/or blowing a gale. There were few entries in the log except to record the occasional memorable dinner party on board, such as when English professors Bengt and Mai Britt and their charming daughter Karin joined me. However, I was completely spoiled by the attentions of Gunne and Eva-Lena who wined and dined me constantly.

There were two notable evenings when a jazz quintet from Gothenberg performed on the main quay, with much participation from musical sailors from the harbour. Much dancing and singing to the old favourites that everyone seemed to know. But it was bitterly cold and raining both evenings. Most people were in their wet weather gear!

Another evening Gunne included me at a supper meeting of the local chapter of the Round Table, which they held on a lighthouse rock island off the coast, and reached by boat from Smogen.

We learned about the geology of Buhusian, and the maritime history of the island, which included an English sailing ship being wrecked on it in a storm with loss of ship, cargo and all hands. One of many lost on the skerries of this coast, before modern navigation aids. As so often in Sweden, the evening ended with a singsong of appropriate local 'oldies'.

The good days were recorded as....

day 21 ✦ *Friday July 16th*

The first nice day since arrival. Took the chance to repair some bad marks in the decks by spot painting with the epoxy paint, and in the afternoon had my first (and only, as it turned out) swim at the Kattesand beach.

day 25 ✦ *Tuesday July 20th*

Woke to the best looking weather for days. Just a little cloud, and a light northerly breeze. Gunne arrived for what had become, not a day of sailing, but a morning coffee time, and moaning about the weather session.

This time he found *Bente* with sails rigged.

Grinning from ear to ear, he clambered aboard and we set off to "go round the island," a normal first exercise. It was a lovely 2 1/2 hour jaunt counterclockwise, in quite variable winds that eventually improved to force 3. Everybody was out sailing that day – there were boats everywhere you looked.

It started to rain again during dinner that evening!

day 28 ✦ *Friday July 23rd*

Sunshine! Gunne was away in Fagersta so I did some essential varnishing, including the gunwhale cap and the rubbing strake which had suffered some minor damage during the trip. Eva-Lena organized a super barbeque for the evening.

Gunne was due back late on the 26th, and we planned to set off together on the 27th to reach Ockero marina before George arrived back on Wednesday the 28th.

day 31 ✧ Monday July 26th

It had started to blow again last night, and not only was there a howl in the rigging, as so often in the last weeks, but the mast was actually shaking.

After a restless night I rose to full gale conditions which were reported later at 20m/s (40 mph). Very few boats ventured out down the partly sheltered island route, one assumes of necessity to return a rental boat or what have you, but with only a small jib hoisted. Not family sailing weather.

On meeting Mai-Britt in the supermarket, she asked if it might be a "Hemingway three-day blow?"

Please not!

The Swedish forecast that evening, at 2150, was for an easing after midday on Tuesday. We ought to be O.K. for tomorrow!

day 32 ✧ Tuesday July 27th

Gunne appeared on schedule at 0845, with the 0700 weather report. It gave wind speed in our area down to 13m/s (26 knots) and rather less to the south toward Gothenberg. After last minute shopping at the handy Konsum supermarket, right beside the marina, we were away by 0945 under double-reefed main, and staysail, for comfort in the fresh southwesterly on our starboard beam.

Bente seemed pleased to be under way again for, with so little sail, she charged along. It seemed best to take the inside passage again even though we would miss some great scenery, but the wind was too southerly and we would have had to tack down some narrow channels using the outside route, in places like Gulhomen and Karingon. The inside route also had some narrows, but was more sheltered and we could motor if necessary.

Before long we were able to start shaking out the reefs, and once through the narrows under the bridge at Vindon we hoisted the yankee and began to tack south down the east side of Orust.

Gunne seemed to be in his element at the helm and never tired of it! By 1430 we reached a narrower part of this route, and the high shores caused a funneling effect which put the falling breeze right on our nose. We downed sails and motored the rest of the way to Stora Byron, arriving there at 1900.

I was determined not to overnight again at Marstrand, and Gunne said he would prefer to discover a new place too.

The harbour was the smallest I had been in on the trip, with barely room to turn *Bente* around, but it looked inviting. There were two or three fishing trawlers, a couple of passenger ferries, a berthing area for residents' boats, and room for perhaps a half dozen visitors.

We must have been number seven, but we did manage to get alongside the jetty squeezed under the bows of a trawler. We were so close that the ensign staff was at risk by the curvature of the trawler's bow.

I took pains to enquire of an onlooker whether they were likely to be going out early in the morning. I felt we might easily be overlooked. But no, the crew were on summer holiday – we could sleep well.

Like almost all the Scandinavian harbours, this one was clean and had excellent facilities ashore, with modern toilets, hot showers, a kiosk, an eating place, and helpful people.

We ate on board in the cockpit, warmed by the bright evening sun, having chicken, rice, cheese, and red wine followed by Weinerbrod cake and coffee. Then a walk across the island which turned out to be about half a mile in diameter, with another harbour at the end of its one road.

There must have been some all year residents from the look of the houses, but the majority would have been owned as second homes for summer holidays. The summers are short up here – they don't start really until early June, and it is 'back to school' mid August.

Annual leave, at least in Sweden, is 6 to 8 weeks so these summer homes are worthwhile. There is some early or late summer rental of homes to 'others', but from a midsummer weekend (around June 21st) until early August, owners are usually in residence.

day 33 ✧ Wednesday July 28th

A rude awakening before 0600 by noisy outboards as young bucks raced their overpowered skiffs in and out of harbour on various errands.

This was supposed to have been a sleeping-in morning, as it would take only about 4 hours to reach Ockero.

Oh, well, it looked to be a nice morning, might as well be up and about.

The sky had only a little cloud, and there was a light breeze, sadly from a southerly direction – no use to us. After using the excellent showers (we had the place to ourselves at that hour) we spoiled ourselves with a cooked breakfast, and then took our leave of this super little place by 0930.

Thumbing our noses at Marstrand as we passed through, we dawdled along casually over the breeze-rippled waters south towards Ockero, enjoying the scenery and the peaceful day.

It was much too soon that we found ourselves there, especially for Gunne I think, for he would be going back to Malmon from here tomorrow.

The harbour was just as empty as before, but shortly after we had berthed, a young man with a pilot's briefcase and a young lady in tow, swung themselves aboard without invitation, and came aft to the cockpit.

When I recovered from surprise, I asked them if they were collecting the marina dues, which seemed the most likely explanation.

"No."

They introduced themselves as customs and immigration officers.

So why had we gone all the way to the ferry terminal office in Gothenberg to report on our arrival?

They avoided my questions about where their office was, and how they found us so promptly. I suspected that some busybody had phoned them and they didn't want to admit that!

Anyway, they filled out their tedious bureaucratic forms, accepted my word that we had no significant amount of foreign booze left, and departed.

I had showed the stamp in my passport, complete with name and phone number of our friendly officer in Gothenberg, and I think they then decided not to mess us around!

This being the last Swedish port of call Gunne helped me to shop for the Swedish specialties that I wanted to take home, and then we went to the local restaurant for an early dinner of pyttipanna (a famous dish of seemingly anything and everything thrown into the frying pan, with delicious results), and after a few beers in the evening sun on their terrace, we wandered back to *Bente*.

Hardly had we climbed aboard when George was there telling us that, incredibly, the bus from the airport had brought him all the way out to Ockero after dropping others off in Gothenberg. I still don't know how he deserved that extraordinary treatment. It was a happy reunion evening.

day 34 ✦ Thursday July 29th

Today would see us back into Danish waters and, hopefully, to Anholt, just over 60 miles away. It had to be an early start, again, leaving Gunne to find his way home by bus to Gothenberg and then train to Malmon. We were away at 0700.

As we motored down the channel we crossed the bows of the ferry departing Ockero for Honno on the mainland, and there was Gunne standing up forward waving us goodbye, a bit sadly, I thought.

He loves sailing and would have continued on with us if he could.

There was a very light breeze from a south-southwesterly direction which was of no use to us, for our course lay due south. The sun was trying to surmount a layer of cloud on the eastern horizon – we might see some sun – but there was more low scud to the west which would be on us before long.

We passed out the main shipping channel, then beside the Trubaduren lighthouse, and settled down for a long day of motoring in the open water of the Kattegat, to Anholt.

It seemed to take forever, and there was little to see to break the monotony, but we promised ourselves a reunion with the good food and pretty waitresses of the harbourside restaurant, as long as we would get there before last orders, which I hoped was 10 p.m.

The hill of Anholt hove into view and we urged *Bente* along, finally reaching harbour at 2100. Taking the first berth we could see, (and the only one) even though it was bow-on to the end of a float with our quarter to the wind, not the best practice, we hustled up to the restaurant. Thankfully, it was still in full swing.

The salmon was as good as last time, as was the service by two quite different lovely blond Danish girls. Where do they all come from?

day 35 ✦ Friday July 30th

Woke to a very strong southwesterly wind, and because we had just secured to our neighbour and not put our anchor out, his anchor had dragged a bit, and we were grinding our bows on the wharf.

In pajamas we launched the rubber dinghy from its position, on deck on the forward end of the cabin trunk, and made ourselves quite wet running out our 5-kilo folding grapnel anchor, on chain and warp, and became independent, to the obvious relief of the skipper beside us!

The forecast on the harbourmaster's notice board offered no relief from the conditions. We gave up hope of being able to make any comfortable progress, even to Grenna, which was 20 miles dead upwind.

We declared a "make and mend", and busied ourselves with refueling, rewatering, reprovisioning, and generally preparing for some long days ahead.

One or two boats did go out under very short sail, turning north toward Gothenberg, and we grabbed the first vacated berth in a nose-into-the-wind position. Our new neighbours, a Dane and his wife, were very pleasant.

In discussing our proposed route south and our rather old and large scale Admiralty chart he said we were suicidal, and ended up selling us several of his new charts that they no longer needed, having themselves finished sailing those waters for the year. The charts would also enable us to return via another route, through the Lille Baelt to the west of Langeland and Fyn, a very beautiful passage.

There were some holiday makers about, trying to enjoy themselves swimming and surfing on the Anholt beaches, but they really did look cold and the waves were crashing dangerously up the shore. We retired later to our favourite restaurant and enjoyed some super steaks off the open grill. One of the waitresses admitted to George that she only recently returned from a couple of years in Sydney, and they began to talk about places they knew. I had to drag him home.

day 36 ✦ Saturday July 31st

Wakened at 0500 by one or two boats getting under way in what sounded like reasonable conditions. We discussed, in our berths, various alternative plans for the day – the ambitious one which was to Ballen on the east side of Samsoe, and the fall-backs of firstly Grenna, and further along, Ebeltoft, which was a little off our route but praised in the pilot book.

Our Danish neighbours had also been awake early and listened to the local Danish weather forecast at 0555, which gave overcast with occasional showers, and winds developing to westerly force 3-4 as the morning advanced. Quite good for our route!

Away we went, hoisting full sail with yankee in what was initially a light northerly breeze, making toward the Jutland shores at Grenna to the southwest, whence we would turn south and on toward Samsoe.

By 1400 the wind had pooped out enough that we had to motor-sail.

Just after the narrows at the north end of Samsoe we were surprised to see a Viking ship, complete with square sail and shields mounted on the gunwales, which passed us going north, and then nosed into a little island and dropped sail, as if it were the most natural thing to do. We were quite taken aback, and imagined all sorts of ancient rites to be performed on that barren shore.

Ballen, the principal harbour on the east side of the island of Samsoe, had become the obvious choice for the night, and we motored in at 1900.

A good size, comparable to Anholt, with the usual ferry facilities on the north side and pleasure boats to the south, it was already full.

In Scandinavia, some yachting families, especially those with children, who want to be sure of a berth, retire to harbour by midafternoon!

We found a spot on the south breakwater with only one boat to scramble over to get ashore. It was a Danish cruiser racer with young lads aboard, so we headed for it in the forthright manner we had learned to use, and were delighted when they rose to take our lines.

It proved to be a very pleasant harbour, with a tiny village, clearly living from the summer holiday trade and the ferry traffic.

As everywhere in Denmark, however, immediately beyond the village one could see fields fully cultivated. There were various holiday makers about, and in the inevitable conversations that ensued, some insisted on believing, maybe because of his appearance, that George was a Sir George. He did little to discourage them.

The lady harbourmistress allowed us to use her phone to report home to England, and this was typical of the atmosphere in this charming little port. Along with a few holiday homes surrounding the harbour, there was a kiosk, a wash house, a delightful looking restaurant, which on investigation proved to be very expensive, and a traveling summer carnival on their little green.

day 37 ✧ Sunday August 1st

What a night!

Firstly, after we had gone to bed listening to the noise and singing of what seemed like a rather large party across the harbour, suddenly we were boarded by the crew of the boat ahead of us, who had decided that our pulpit was too close to their pushpit, and they were going to overhaul my docking lines.

Well, I soon took over that exercise!

Then, at 0200, a little German boat crewed by two exhausted but polite young men came alongside, so I was up to help them secure to us.

Danes are known to be rather prolific drinkers on occasion, and it was, after all, Saturday night. The revelries went on, and on, seemingly all night.

Struggling up at 0630 we went up to the office of the harbourmistress to examine the 0600 forecast which she had promised would be posted by then. It wasn't. Somebody must have overslept. Or, more probably, life is taken just that little bit more casually in out-of-the-way places like this.

We met some other sailors up at the wash house who said they had a forecast of winds southwest of 12 m/s (24 knots) and then added, "or more." I didn't follow that comment because forecasts aren't normally given in that way.

Anyway, it meant that the course to go via the Lille Baelt would be dead upwind through narrowing channels, and thus quite hopeless. We sadly resigned ourselves to go back the way we had come along the east side of Langeland.

Our favourite little island of Omo would make too short a trip to stop there, and we chose to head for the tiny port of Spodsberg, about two thirds of the way down the east side of Langeland – in fact, the only harbour on that side.

We apologetically woke the very tired German boys alongside us and were away at 0715, with double-reefed main and staysail, into the already stiff southwesterly.

The engine was used to give us more drive to windward, because we had to pass to weather of a buoy marking the western end of a serious reef, some miles south of Samsoe.

The Navstar proved its worth again when we made the reef buoy a waypoint, and we read off the course to steer, and compared that to the compass course we could make, without pinching too hard.

It was going to be touch and go!

As we worked our way south away from the lee of Samsoe into open water the waves became quite choppy, but *Bente* took it very comfortably.

The mark was cleared without having to tack, and then we were in clear water and able to ease off a bit, and dispense with the engine. Then we aimed for the bulge in the land north of Kerteminde which, when reached, would shelter us from the seas for quite a while.

Eventually we passed the headland to the north of Kerteminde Bay, and eased to a broad reach toward the channel through the bridge construction work off Korsor.

The wind had eased a little and we had a good sail, gradually shaking out the reefs and hoisting the small jib as we mock-raced some others who had emerged from Kerteminde Bay.

After passing through the bridge-causeway project, at about 1300, we found a wind hole so put the motor on to cross the ferry lane as quickly as possible. A nice breeze returned, from more westerly, and stayed with us for most of the afternoon as we coasted down just off the shore of Langeland, reaching Spodsberg at 1800.

The pilot book had said it was a tiny little harbour and added "Moor outside if you have to, but beware the wash from the ferry boats coming and going into the adjacent harbour."

A timely warning, because we had to dodge one when it came out and turned around in front of us as we motored toward the boat harbour!

Well, yes, the harbour was tiny, and full, but just as we entered a motor cruiser cast off from the main breakwater-dock on the south side and it was a perfect fit for *Bente*!

It was a lovely setting of blue sky, gentle breeze, and sun setting over this quaint little out-of-the-way place. We treated ourselves to snaps, salmon in cream sauce, new potatoes, and red wine, with George doing great service over the paraffin stove.

These were usually the moments when we reflected on the day's events, especially when the sailing had been as good as today, and when we had enjoyed other things, like the large fish we had seen jumping just south of Samsoe. The locals later told us that they might have been porpoise, which were known to be around in small numbers.

Our after-dinner walkabout revealed a tiny settlement with a few fishermen's cabins around the harbour, a wash house, ferry terminal, and little else. Looking down the coast road we could see some houses and a petrol station, so the 'berg' must have been down there.

day 38 ✧ Monday August 2nd

We woke to clear skies! And just a light breeze, from the southeast.

Good for today's leg, but a strange direction. I wondered what significance it had in this part of the world, but didn't bother to enquire.

With the plastic 10-litre diesel containers in hand we wandered down the road, but found that the petrol station didn't have diesel. That was a surprise! Are there so few diesel cars in Denmark? Anyway, there was a supermarket, so we stocked up on bread, milk, and some lovely Danish pastries.

They advised that diesel was available on the harbourside where the few fishing boats were secured, but that we would have to get ahold of the Harbourmaster who worked at the ferry ticket office. We found out that he wouldn't be available until *sometime* later in the day. Finally, we gave up, knowing we had enough to last until Kiel or beyond, depending on how much we used the engine.

Roused the crews of the two large German boats which had come in after us last evening, and secured in the only place available, which was rafting outside us. I was surprised that they were able to come in because their draft was surely greater than ours and I thought we had just made it!

Away by 0815, and by the time the sails were up, the breeze had improved to almost force 3. The direction was steady and we could, by staying as high as possible, just clear the end of Langeland without broaching ourselves on a course of 190 degrees.

Even close-hauled we were making 5 to 6 knots, soon cleared Langeland, and eased off to 225 degrees toward the lighthouse off Kiel, and barreled along in what was the best sail so far on the cruise.

There were quite a few boats sailing, most of them German boats heading north for their traditional August holiday in Scandinavia when the harbours are not so congested, because the natives have gone back to work.

Passing the lighthouse, we sailed on past the Kiel Yacht Club, preferring instead to spend the night in the small mooring area just to starboard of the lock entrance.

Suddenly we were hailed by a Halberg Rassy 29 with a Canadian Forces crew on board, who had spotted our Canadian ensign, and made a bee line to us to chat us up. On holiday from their base in Germany, they had borrowed the boat from the British Forces Yacht club, just north of the canal entrance.

It was a squeeze to get into the mooring area after again persuading some reluctant Germans to move enough to let us in. Quickly then, over to the chart shop I remembered on the east side of the locks, which fortunately was open until 2100.

I bought two charts I wanted to complete my information for the Elbe-Frisian Islands passage. They were the access to Norderney's little harbour, in case we needed shelter there, and the route to Harlingen in Between Terschelling and Vileland, for the same reason.

Back at *Bente* we found a Swedish 38-footer rafted along side us, and we directed the skipper and his crew, his wife, to the chart office. They were bound for the Mediterranean via the French canals and had no charts or tide tables from here to France! He also admitted a draft of 1.90 metres, but added that a friend had made it through with 2 metres. I wondered what trials they would face!

day 39 ✧ Tuesday August 3rd

The Holtenau lock opened for business, for pleasure craft at least, at 0700, and we were there ready to go. Our hope was to get through the canal in time to catch the last of the ebb and carry it the 20 miles down to Cuxhaven before dark. If we could get through the canal without delay, it should take just 11 hours, so it was theoretically possible.

Along we went, checking our progress against the kilometre posts on the canal bank. There had been a fuelling station near Rendsburg, but it seemed to have been closed down. Anyway, although it would have been convenient and timely, I was just as happy not to use up any precious minutes.

In late afternoon, the weather, which had been reasonable enough, with a light crossbreeze and cumulus clouds, suddenly looked quite nasty, with very black clouds to the southwest of us. There was a squall or two accompanied by rain. It looked like a front going through, but the track seemed to be northeastward, and there was lighter sky ahead of us to the south.

Fingers crossed!

Right on schedule, at 1800, we arrived at the Brunsbuttel lock.

We just missed locking through with some boats a mile or so ahead of us, so we circled around in the approaches making it as obvious as possible that we wanted in.

Nothing happened for ages.

I could see that the lock had emptied.

Finally, in exasperation, I called up the local lock control on their frequency, only to find myself listening to music!

Then I tried Kiel Canal central control and explained my wish to catch the tide, and the music problem.

Well, I don't know much German, but when I turned back to the local frequency, the fur was really flying, and the lock was open in minutes!

It was 1915 when we were clear and the ebb was flowing with a vengeance. We reached Cuxhaven in under 2 1/2 hours, making 9 knots over the ground at one point, and we carefully aimed into the yacht harbour to avoid being swept past by the still very fast running tide.

No sooner had we secured in about the only berth I could see, than the harbourmaster was there telling us to move because that row of berths was reserved for boats over 11 metres. (*Bente* is 10.5 metres.) "Couldn't you read the sign on the dockside behind?"

What a twerp he was!

Finally it was settled by me offering to pay the fee applicable to the larger boat, and he left.

There was no way I was going to move!

day 40 ✧ Wednesday August 4th

The Ro-Ro terminal next to the yacht basin had been inactive during the night so we could enjoy a reasonable sleep. Our next step had already been determined by the tide, because we had to wait for the start of the ebb to enable us to get out of the Elbe and its estuary.

A local skipper advised us that to get full benefit we should leave the basin just before slack water, and that would mean 1400 hours. Thus we had a convenient morning to refuel and shop. The yacht club didn't have any fuel station, I knew, so we took the plastic cans and walked a mile to the nearest petrol station, and took a taxi back.

A visit to the nearby Marine Met Office found the pleasant duty officer just back from his holidays, and not familiar with recent weather patterns. He gave us a very conditional opinion of the short and longer term outlook, based on the weather chart issued that morning.

He didn't think there were any storms in the offing, but he couldn't be sure!

On that information we felt our best course was not to attempt to go for Den Helder now, but go first to Helgoland 35 miles away, review the weather, and from there Den Helder would be 150 miles.

Quite a few boats left as we did, and motorsailed down the river, close-hauled in the light southwest wind. Most were larger, so soon left us behind, but we made excellent time for the first few hours.

There was some horrible wind over tide chop later on that we hammered through very uncomfortably. It slowed us down enough that we did not make it all the way to Helgoland on the ebb, and had the increasing flood right on our nose.

The last few miles took forever. We were back in big tide waters!

It was dark as we approached, trying to sort out the lights we needed from those of the town behind, but finally we entered behind the high stone walls defending the harbour from the ravages of the North Sea.

day 41 ✧ Thursday August 5th

What a relief it was to escape from Helgoland! This little sandhill with its protected harbour looks inviting enough after a day at sea, but those high black stone walls seemed to do more than just keep out the North Sea. They were positively intimidating!

When we arrived the night before, hungry and tired after a longer and more bumpy than expected crossing, we found the inner harbour very crowded.

Perhaps we should have simply dropped anchor in the outer harbour for the night, but no one else had done so, and I wanted to go ashore in the morning to consult the weather office, before our trip across the North Sea to Den Helder.

As we headed gingerly for what looked like a sensible berthing space a megaphoned voice struck us out of the lights and shadows ashore, saying, *"Don't go there!"*

It could only be addressed to us because nothing else was moving. Confused by the contradiction of logic I shouted back, 'Why not?' and the voice replied *"Because I say so!"* And we were ordered alongside a raft of sailboats already about 12 deep from the jetty.

Very unsafe, and climbing over 12 boats to get ashore was impossible.

As we secured our lines to the outermost boat, which had arrived only minutes before us, the skipper warned us that some Dutch boats closer to the jetty would be leaving at first light, and we would have to get up then to cast off and reorganize the raft.

Oh boy, a short night ahead!

The Dutch must have overslept, or felt a bit of conscience, because it was all of 0530 when shouts and knocking on our cabin side announced the reorganization.

Once up and about, George and I looked at each other with understanding and set about to make our own departure. But we had not cleared the inner harbour before the harbourmaster's megaphone was blaring again, calling us by name to come and pay harbour dues.

For what? I wondered.

Anyway, to avoid any complications we nosed over and I climbed the ladder up the horrible stone wall and paid the ransom.

When I asked about the weather report and charts, he explained in mixed German and English that the Met Office wasn't open til 0900. I overheard on his radio in the background what I thought was a gale warning, but when I queried it, he said,

'*Die veder ist O.K. – no gales!*'

Out we went, with no looking back! There was a very useful south-easterly breeze – just what we needed.

At our target speed of 5 knots we would cover the 150 miles in 30 hours and arrive in Den Helder around midday tomorrow, Friday. We could be back home by the weekend.

With only a minor departure from the lay line course we would converge with the Frisian Islands somewhere before Borkum, and then we could skirt them as before, using the inshore main channel markers to guide us. There would also be big beacons on each island to mark our progress.

The breeze held all morning and on a beam reach we were making a good six knots, but it began to ease about midday, and nearing 1400 we thought we should use the engine to keep up our speed.

George offered to first go below and tune in the 1355 marine forecast, now that we were again in range of B.B.C. longwave.

We really ought to have listened to the morning forecast at 0550, but in the process of leaving Helgoland, we missed it.

The typical disinterested B.B.C. voice was almost a pleasure to hear after a month away, but suddenly my ears perked up. The synopsis said something about gales and the German Bight area, which was where we were.

We listened intently as the detailed report confirmed, "German Bight, gale south west force 8, imminent!"

What a kick in the stomach that was!

Almost if by a signal from the radio, the wind died completely, and presented an eerie glassy sea under the solid grey sky. We both now recognized the signs which confirmed the forecast.

So, first on with the engine, which was always a comfort, and then I went below to assess our situation, and decide what was best to do.

The nearest shelter was the yacht haven at the west end of Borkum. The approach via the Westerems channel was 20 miles south west of us – right up wind of the forecast gales.

The alternatives were to return to Helgoland, some 7 to 8 hours in a gale to that horrible place – no thank you!

Then there was Norderney, some 25 miles due east, but that would be a step backwards.

It was decided by the tide which was ebbing westward down the islands at about 1 to 1/2 knots. This would enable us to make 5 to 6 knots towards Borkum, compared to maybe 4 to 5 knots backwards to Norderney.

So Borkum it would be, with a prayer that the build up of the seas would be slow enough to let us reach the Westerems buoy, some 3 to 3 1/2 hours upwind. After which our course would be east of south up the river Ems channel, with another 12 miles to the marina at Borkum, but the seas would then be aft of the beam and quite manageable.

The eerie-looking, oily sea was first of all traced with 'cat's paws' of breeze from the southwest, then ripples, wavelets, and then progressively larger and larger waves as the wind increased.

We watched the Navstar anxiously as it reported speed over ground and distance to go. Initially, we were making over six knots, but as the pounding increased, we slowed to 5 1/2 and then 5 knots.

The tide was helping us along even if it probably increased the choppiness of the seas in opposition. It was now very windy and the seas quite staggering, but we knew we had a sound ship, and it was clear that we were making it, and we rounded the buoy, with a little cheer, at 1715.

The run up the channel was straightforward. I had set the waypoint on a key buoy out of sight several miles ahead, and we aimed for that until we could pick up the port and starboard hand marks of the channel.

All around us was a mass of white raging hills of water, breaking into turmoil as it reached the shallow sandbanks ahead on each side.

The staysail might have helped to steady our motion and increase our speed a little, but we were doing quite well and I didn't want to risk damaging it, or me, on the foredeck!

The town with its large beachfront apartments was in view to port as we made our way up channel against the last of the ebb. Still no shelter from the seas in the wide estuary, but up ahead we could now see the tower on the tip of the long breakwater.

We reached it at 2000, and turned into calm water with the wind still raging over our heads.

About a half mile ahead we could see some masts, meaning marina and sanctuary, and we peered for the crevice in the sand dunes which was its tiny entrance.

Finally, there it was, and we turned in – and came to a full stop.

Aground in the sand!

It was low water, but there was supposed to be at least 2 metres depth throughout the marina. What a strange twist!

We laughed as we dropped the anchor and broke out the Southern Comfort. We were ashore.

People from the marina gathered on the bank of the entrance to enjoy the spectacle, and make jokes about our predicament, but it was already low water so we wouldn't become 'high and dry' and after an hour the flood eased us free and we moved into the harbour.

It was very windswept because the whole island is just a sandbank, but the perimeter had been built up a little. The docks were quite new and rugged in typical German fashion, and for a change there was plenty of room.

It was 2200 when we were secure, and then some food and off to bed, tired but satisfied with our day's achievement.

day 42 ✦ Friday August 6th

The gale blew all night. *Bente* was beam to the pontoon, with the usual breast ropes and springs, but the wind always sounds worse when I am below at night, so in the wee hours I went up top and put an anchor warp around a main piling. Then I could sleep.

Morning found the wind as strong as ever from the west, and now it was raining as well.

A look around showed a half-full marina with a mixture of motor and sail yachts, including a Sadler 29 from England, but there were few people around. A newish building was obviously the office, and seemed to have a restaurant above, but beyond that there was nothing to be seen but sand. We straggled up to the office and found super showers, and phones to call home.

The harbourmaster confirmed that there was no fuelling facility, he had no weather information, and that the fee would by DM 22.50 for the night. German harbours always seemed more expensive, and less well equipped, than in Scandinavia.

George and I talked about what to do next. Clearly we would not be able to go outside the Frisian Islands today, or maybe even tomorrow. Staying here was a pretty dismal prospect. We decided to take the route through Holland to Den Helder, as we had done for the same reason in 1990 and had quite enjoyed.

George was wanting to get home, and wasn't keen on the extra 2 or 3 days this would take, but at least we would be progressing, so he didn't complain.

The canal system starts at Delfjil some 20 miles up the River Ems from here, and the flood tide would start about 0830. We had breakfast and set off at 0930.

The route out beside the breakwater was into the wind, but sheltered from the seas. At its end, the combination of wind, waves, and strong tide made it rather tense until we squeaked past the turning mark, clear of the leeward sandbanks, and into the main channel of the river, and turned tail to it all.

We went very, very fast!

It was surely over 10 knots, and the channel marks had huge wakes as they leaned in the now full flood.

There was commercial traffic to avoid, but otherwise hardly a care in the world, except to wonder how we could turn in behind the Delfjil breakwater without being swept past.

A careful study of the detail chart I had fortuitously bought against just this turn of events, enabled me to edge out of the channel to make the turn a little easier, and at 1100 we were in still water.

There was no need to go into the marina up ahead near the town and we went straight to the canal entrance where we called up the control on V.H.F. and were told we could enter in 15 minutes.

While in the lock I checked in at the little customs office for good order's sake – with a Canadian ensign and so on – but they took my word that we were British residents and didn't want to know anything beyond that.

Then we were away, heading west along the large straight canal, much used by commercial traffic, toward Groningen. The few bridges along the way opened as we approached, and most seem now operated from some central office – I suppose using T.V. cameras to see the traffic.

We were not delayed until we reached the eastern edge of Groningen. There the bridge was closed, and we couldn't raise any response on V.H.F., so we moored alongside the bank to await developments.

Two young Dutchmen in the sailboat ahead of us had overheard our V.H.F. inquiry, and came along to explain the situation of opening times and problems of staff shortages. Then, using our V.H.F., they called up central office and obtained their agreement to take us through to the Sudhafen, in the center of town, before closing down for the night at 1900 hours.

As the weekend was now upon us, we knew we would have a slower passage ahead of us, and would have to read our Dutch almanac carefully re bridge and lock opening times to avoid unexpected and frustrating delays.

We had now turned off from the main commercial canal, because of its low fixed bridges, which would have required our mast being unstepped. The canal we would use all the way to Leeuwarden was the original, old, narrow, shallow but picturesque one, which had many locks and bridges all operated for the benefit of pleasure craft, and therefore a bit more casually.

The canal is supposed to offer a 2-metre minimum depth, but even with our 1.70 metre draft we were advised in 1990 to stay in the middle, and quite often we felt ourselves slowing down as we plowed through the mud, and twice we became quite stuck. There is control of water levels, at least in some sections, but we were told that wet weather is helpful!

The Sudhafen, with its well-preserved brick-walls topped by a line of trees, and brick roadways for access to the tall stately homes just behind, was a picture, and was also full of residential barges and other boats in every permitted place.

Our one attempt to secure alongside a barge left us stuck in the mud. Finally a lock keeper, seeing our plight, told us we could go alongside in a restricted place as long as we would be away promptly in the morning, and wouldn't obstruct traffic.

With *Bente's* mast in a tree, and her keel in the mud, we settled down for the night.

day 43 ✦ Saturday August 7th

Strange to wake up in such a beautiful and unique situation. Up through the trees were some patches of blue sky between fast-moving cloud. It looked like the cold front had passed, and we could expect settled weather of the day with fresh westerly wind and maybe an occasional shower.

A bit of exploration ashore found us a super bread shop, with all the sweet cakes one could dream of. However, this was a rather more industrial end of this beautiful university town, and there weren't any other shops or restaurants, and the scenery would be even more beautiful as we progressed.

The scheduled 0900 opening of the next bridge, which was really a series of bridges close one after the other in the centre of the town, was delayed a half hour to await a convoy joining from the Oosthafen.

There was only one bridge operator, and he had to travel along with us, opening and closing each bridge as we passed through. Then he would hurtle past us on his bicycle to the next one. Meanwhile each boat in the long file had to move the short distance and then idle in the water, trying to keep station, until the next bridge was opened.

The last bridge on the outside of town was a railway bridge – famous for causing delay – and so it was – 40 minutes for little apparent reason, except I suppose, waiting for a sufficient gap in their schedule of trains to be sure no train would ever be slowed down by the bridge being open.

Another one-hour delay further along when a bridge operator was away at his lunch. Then the most testing stretch of winding, narrow, shallow canal which was probably a river at one time. Carefully we followed the middle course, and held our breath when we moved aside to pass or be passed. Most passers were Dutch, and all were pleasant as they went by.

Finally, the canal began to widen and we emerged into the openness of the Lauersmeer. We still followed the buoyed channel, but there were many shallow draft centerboard boats out enjoying Saturday's fresh breeze as they criss-crossed the lake.

Some beautiful barges in full sail came across our path from the sea toward the Dokkum Canal, and we turned to port to follow them. Gradually the route ahead narrowed, and we moved from lake back into canal.

It really is a most scenic route through Holland. The winding canals passing through farms with crops, then cattle, then ducks and swans on the water, then passing through some little village with old buildings down to the water edge, a lifting or swinging bridge, maybe a lock, old but well-maintained, and a lock keeper's precious flower beds. Always something to see and appreciate.

Dokkum appeared ahead of us at 1900, and as expected, its first bridge was closed for the night. We could go no further.

On the canal bank to port was a fuel station – how convenient! The first we had seen in the canals. We topped up, and then moved along till we found a vacant cruiser that we could secure to, and be a little out from the bank for better depth.

Dinner started with mustard sild and green salad, followed by tinned ham and boiled new potatoes washed down with gulps of a full-bodied Australian red, then cakes from this morning's shop, and the inevitable coffee. After that we needed a walkabout in the little town. It was quaint, but seemed empty of life, so after a phone call home, we rejoined our ship.

day 44 ✧ Sunday August 8th

Overslept the B.B.C. forecast again! Oh well, we hardly need it here. Scrambled eggs, bread, cheese, jam and coffee prepared us for another day, and promptly at 0900 the bridge began to open. A sailing barge ahead of us cast off and headed through. As fast as we could we set off in pursuit, but the bridge started to close.

We hollered in dismay, and then got out our loud compressed air cylinder fog horn.

Well, they heard that! The bridge began to reopen to let us through. Perhaps the barge had been in radio contact, and no one expected us, or saw us tagging along behind.

Three bridges later we were clear of Dokkum and away toward Leeuwarden, enjoying another leisurely dawdle through the farms of Friesland in some rather pleasant weather. It was along this Dokkum that they practiced the gimmick of seeking tips for opening each bridge, and do it by putting a wooden shoe on the end of a fishing rod line, so that you can drop coins in as you go past. At some places they even have a sign to indicated how much is expected. One is well advised to have a goodly supply of Guilder coins before trying to go through.

All went well until we reached the outskirts of Leeuwarden about 1300 and were stopped by a bridge which wouldn't reopen until 1700. There were already two or three Dutch sailboats waiting against the canal bank, and we were welcomed alongside one of them.

The prospect for getting all the way to Harlingen that evening was the main topic of conversation. Once past this bridge we would have only 2 hours before normal 1900 close down, but maybe the last stretch of canal after Leeuwarden would be open later because it was a main commercial route?

The bridge at Franeker was the last one before Harlingen, and it was about a 2-hour run ahead. In the event, the faster boats of our little group just made it through, and we didn't by 3 minutes. No amount of wailing would help. The keeper had gone to tea. So our destiny was Franeker – another day lost. Frustration!

And a grey, boring, industrial town to boot. No diversion there.

day 45 ✧ Monday August 9th

The end of the Harinxma Canal was reached by late morning, and, unusually, the gates of the last lock were both open. We shot right through into the main harbour of Harlingen. I guess at that time the sea level was the same as that of the canal, or they were adding a little water to the canal system.

There was a stiff west wind blowing outside, and anyway the tide was wrong, so going on to Den Helder was not an option. Knowing Harlingden to be a super harbour and town to visit, we were happy as we turned to port, through the bridge and lock gates, into the inner harbour.

Why not enjoy ourselves with a bit of shopping, have a good meal ashore, research the weather outlook, and if all is well, set off tomorrow with the tide to Den Helder, our last stop before crossing to the River Deben?

Checking in with the harbourmaster's office in the chandlery, we saw that morning's forecast. Would you believe it? Gales and rain for the next two days.

Nothing to do but grin and bear it, but at least we were in this beautiful place with much to see and many good restaurants. There had been a berth for us alongside the wall of the long narrow yacht harbour, so it was easy to come and go.

Originally this must have been the entrance to the canal system, but now it came to a dead end with the yacht harbour, and was replaced, I suppose, by the Harinxma Canal. The harbour was therefore right in the middle of town, and it was only a few steps to everything.

The harbourmaster must have been surprised when I came to his shop to pay my dues because from the absence of markers on their pulpits, few other boats (visitors, mostly German) bothered to pay, and he didn't seem to go out of his way to collect. Perhaps the city fathers felt it was enough to have their custom in the restaurants and shops.

Anyway, he was very helpful, and allowed us to use his fax machine to receive the British Met Office three and five day forecasts that my son in London agreed to send us each day until we could get away.

day 46 ✧ Tuesday August 10th

The day passed with much reading down below to stay out of the wind and rain. A visit to the local museum was a fascinating diversion, and the excellent sea food dinner ashore that evening went down very well.

The harbour had filled up during the day as those who came in to escape the bad weather added to those who, like us, decided to stay put. There were two others rafted outboard of us, but they had lines ashore so all was under control. The harbour was tidal, of course, and some care was taken with lines to allow for the nearly 2-metre rise and fall.

day 47 ✧ Wednesday August 11th

Blowing very hard from the west, with the rain merely varying in intensity. It was worth seeing, so I went out to the harbour control tower, where there was a good view over the outer harbour to the Waddensee beyond, and watched a big 50 foot police vessel helping several boats which had ventured out in it and of course were soon in distress.

Some people were trying to get to Harlingen, and possibly the canal's entrance, from Terschelling, which seemed to be a popular holiday destination. The long channel from there was well marked, and the trip was a broad reach, so perhaps possible for the right boat well-handled.

But most of these boats were being sailed by families! I watched with concern as the lifeboat crew arrived in response to a summons, and manned their shallow-draft motor launch and the high-powered two man inflatable, and go charging off into the murk. Before long a sailboat of about 30 feet hove into view in tow of the launch, with the inflatable's crew manning it, as the owner and wife huddled below, exhausted, and very frightened.

They had been blown sideways out of control across the channel, and a long way bumping across the sand shallows downwind, before help arrived. The police launch had seen them go, fortunately, but was too deep a draft to help, and had radioed for the lifeboat.

It was a very good illustration of the wisdom of staying put in harbour in that weather. In the early afternoon, before high tide, the control lock into the inner harbour had to be closed, because the wind had pushed the water level over a metre higher than normal, and facilities inside would not be able to handle it.

The horrible weather was forgotten for a couple of hours that evening, when George and I retired to a pasta restaurant, which we found was run by an Italian family, and they really knew how to prepare tagliatelle. Their Chianti was pretty good, too!

The weather was supposed to be better tomorrow, good enough at least to slip over to Den Helder, which, with the tide, should only take about five hours. A high pressure area centered west of England would progressively dominate conditions, and bring west to northwest winds.

We were impatient to get under way again.

day 48 ✦ Thursday August 12th

The Dutch forecast was put in the window at 0900, and that from my son arrived minutes later, and both warned of a force 8 gale that day. A small, deep depression was sliding up from Biscay along the French coast, and looked to be a real nasty!

Well, that was it! George had had enough, and wanted to return to England, and I was tired, too, and would enjoy a few days of home comforts.

George was never very confident in any met office predictions anyway, and said I would be wiser to wait until the present period of unsettled weather passed and something more near stability returned.

Two very helpful young ladies in a travel office managed to book us by train from Harlingen that afternoon, connecting with the evening ferry from Hook of Holland to Harwich, which would have us into London by train mid-morning on Friday.

The harbourmaster kindly agreed to berth *Bente* in the little marina area of the harbour, and keep an eye on her, for the week or so that I would be away.

It was with a feeling of relief when we boarded the train that afternoon. But it was also mixed with sadness for leaving *Bente,* and a silly feeling of embarrassment for abandoning the cruise, even if it was only an interruption.

day 49 ✧ Friday August 13th

I'm not very superstitious, but it was just as well to have both feet on dry land today!

George and I parted, with strange feelings after all we had been through together, at Waterloo station.

From then on the embarrassment of arriving home by train became much stronger, but I consoled myself by anticipating the pleasure of a hot bath and my large soft bed, and a little of being spoiled by my wife, after seven weeks afloat.

But *Bente* had to be brought home, so that afternoon I was busy phoning a delivery skipper who might do it, with or without my help.

I thought Hugh Lamb, who had surveyed *Bente* last autumn, and was well-known on the East Coast might recommend one, or at least give a reference on one I had come up with. Out of the blue Hugh said,

"Why don't you ask my son Charles to help you bring her back? He has experience beyond his 24 years, including a trans-Atlantic with his mother and sister. And he is unemployed, so is available."

I then spoke to Charles, and it was all fixed for about a week hence, the exact timing to depend on the general weather outlook.

day 58 ✧ Sunday August 22nd

The rendezvous was in the boarding area of the ferry terminal in the early afternoon for a 1500 departure.

Charles found me in my distinctive blue and yellow splashdown jacket, and after introducing himself, sheepishly told me that he had forgotten his passport, but his mother was bringing it round from their home in Shotley, right across on the other side of the river.

Keeping an eye upon the front of the terminal and the car park, we waited as the time for departure came closer. With one hour to go, I began to wonder, and began making enquiries among ferry staff, while Charles phoned home again.

She was bringing it over in the rubber dinghy with outboard!

At 15 minutes to go a ferry security officer admitted that some lady in a dinghy had been trying to land alongside the ferry, but was told she couldn't – that berthing fees for any vessel were £3000!

Can anyone believe such nonsense!

I blew my top and told the security chap to have someone accept the passport from the lady or else!

At the very last possible moment some other staff member appeared and asked quite nonchalantly,

"Is anyone looking for a passport?" I didn't know whether to kick him or kiss him.

Charles turned out to be a fascinating young man – a history graduate from a Welsh university, and thus rather unemployable in commercially oriented occupations, but he was busy creating a classic boat from a skeleton in his front yard. He was also a vegetarian and a smoker. Oh, well!

We were the only passengers on the train as it reached Harlingen, the end of the line, at midnight. The town was deserted and we walked to the harbour, with bags, by dead reckoning.

Bente had been moved to another berth, but a quick check found it well done, and we were soon settled in.

day 59 ✧ Monday August 23rd

The Met Office forecast in England before I left had suggested better weather coming, with generally more stable conditions. The harbour-master's forecast for the day was westerly force 4 to 5.

After shopping for food supplies (especially to cover the vegetarian requirement) we set off late morning, just before high tide, to have benefit of the ebb tide for as long as possible.

There was lots of company, from full rigged barges to little sailing cruisers, for barely two people, as we charged along under full sail on a beam reach southward. But many of them left us to lock into the Zuider Zee as we turned west to beat up the wide channel toward Texel.

A little help from the engine saw us around the weather mark, and then we eased off onto a beam reach again toward Den Helder. It was a great sail, and a good initiation for the new team.

The yacht club staff were as welcoming as they had been in late June, and we later enjoyed some of the simple fare in the café upstairs.

An elderly English couple had arrived just before dark, in their lovely new Bowman 40, having come *that day* the outside route all the way from Borkum. They admitted a very long and tiring day, and I admired their courage, and their fine ship. They said that their main worry as they motored along had been the proximity of the sand shoals to leeward during most of their rough trip. But what a difference it can make when you can do over 7 knots compared to our 5 1/2 under power!

Another arrival in the harbour that day was a 25-foot sloop owned by a young Danish boat builder who had trained in England, and finished off a partly-built wooden boat for himself while in his first job at Snape, and then decided to go home. He had been crewed across the North Sea by his ex-boss, the manager of the wooden boat builder at Snape, who was returning home the next day.

Charles and I were very disappointed to learn that the Dutch weather forecast for the next day was for high winds and heavy rain.

All we could do was review after the next morning's B.B.C. shipping forecast.

day 60 ✦ Tuesday August 24th

So it was, blowing a gale, and teeming with rain. So much for the Met Office 3 and 5 day forecasts which I had obtained on Friday and which had been so optimistic!

It was a thoroughly miserable, wet day, but at least we had a long meeting in *Bente* with the young Dane (and his ex-boss) to tell him what he faced ahead, and I think we persuaded him to route through the Dutch canals to Borkum, and then through the Kiel canal, rather than his vague plan of putting to sea and heading north east until he hit Denmark!

He had almost no charts for the way ahead, so I sold him mine for a song, and threw in a spare copy of the *Baltic Southwest Pilot*.

Our discomfort at being stuck in Den Helder was heightened when we were told that from the third day the dues doubled to discourage long stayers.

There would only be about one hour of ebb tide remaining when we could tune in the 0550 B.B.C. shipping forecast (0655 in Den Helder). A quick decision would have to be made if we were to get through the gap and out to sea before the tide turned against us.

We woke early and made everything as ready as possible, with even the dock lines singled up.

'German Bight, Humber, Thames, west to northwest force 4 to 5, occasional showers...."

We looked at each other and Charles said, "We probably won't get any better this month," so we went for it!

Motoring out even with the tide it seemed to take forever to clear the gap, but eventually we could turn south west down the wide buoyed channel toward deep water, and make sail.

We set a waypoint on a cardinal buoy on Brown's shoal about 60 miles or halfway, and on the lay line and settled down. The wind was quite light at first, barely a force three, but it increased steadily all morning, as did the seas – sometimes long sweeps, and then periods of horribly steep chop. There were huge black clouds coming at us, one after another, bringing rain and wind squalls to keep us on our toes.

By midday we felt it was at the top of force 5, and had put in a reef and took down the jib. It was a close reach, with the waves pretty much on our beam, so we were still making between 5 and 6 knots under reduced sail.

At 1355 I sent Charles below to tune in the B.B.C. shipping forecast, and he returned to the cockpit to report stronger winds in some areas, but much the same as last forecast for sea areas Humber, where we were now, and Thames ahead of us. (It was much later that he admitted that the forecast for our area had been revised to force 5 to 6, locally 7, but he had not wanted to worry me unnecessarily!)

Well, it had become quite a bouncy trip, and the North Sea was a mess of white horses tumbling at us from the north west. Luckily they came to our beam, and with reduced sail *Bente* was coping very well. I recalled being told by an experienced skipper that boats could usually take more than their crew! An oil platform to leeward had waves breaking high up its legs, and much spray.

The cardinal buoy, or way point, appeared right where it should be, at 1700. We were making a very good 6 knots average. The next waypoint was set on the Shipwash light vessel off Orford, and once there we would be practically home. The question was – how would we handle the night hours when some sleep would be necessary?

Obviously, we were short-handed for these conditions. One man on watch to steer, and he couldn't leave the helm to do any chart work, or attend to the sails or anything that might need attention. There was 65 miles to go to the Shipwash light, say 12 hours, and this late in the season, and in these conditions, it would be dark for probably 7 of them.

Charles rather bravely, but foolishly, volunteered to steer all night if necessary – which of course nobody could have done safely.

I decided that the best thing to do was to set up the Autohelm, and put on the engine to give constant positive steerage, to ease the load on it and provide all the electric power we would need for it and navigation lights, etc. We had already put in the second reef in the main, and with that and the small staysail, *Bente* should not have any problems unless conditions became much worse.

Charles doubted that the Autohelm would be able to take the strain, and had experienced failures in the past, when automobile steering would burn out, but I was a little more confident, and anyway we might as well try it.

This way we could stand watch under the shelter of the spray hood, keeping dry and out of the wind, and just keep an eye on the compass inches from your nose, to make sure the Autohelm was O.K., and watch out for shipping and hazards.

After a meal of hot soup, cheese, pate, biscuits, and chocolate, we settled down to a 2-hour watch rota – there wouldn't be any proper sleep, but we should avoid becoming too cold or overtired.

Charles said, much later, that he was surprised how comfortable it was in the leeward bunk, snugged in with the lee cloth, and that he was hardly aware of what was going on up top. *Bente* being of such deep design, the bunks are below water level, and the motion down there, even in these conditions, was relatively gentle.

Some of the shipping routes were already behind us, but we still had the southbound main route, and of course all of the British inshore traffic to watch out for during the night. It was fortunate that visibility range was quite good. Course alterations such as to get through a fleet of fishing trawlers, were by push button on the autohelm control box in the after end of the cockpit, reached comfortably with safety harness hooked on to the main points beside the companionway.

It was quite a night, with those large seas, often topped by a breaking white horse, sometimes rearing up suddenly in a mad way, wind howling through the rigging, spray flying such that even under the spray hood you ducked involuntarily, and still those big black clouds coming at us, relentlessly bringing rain and squalls in between. There was sometimes a glimpse of the stars, which was somehow a comfort.

At 0100 I picked up faint flashes of the Orfordness light, which we knew had a range of 30 miles. That was encouraging – now we had a homing beacon!

Just before first light a northbound ship on a collision course made a major alteration to starboard to pass astern of us, so clearly our radar reflector did the job, because we wouldn't have been very visible in these conditions, even if they had a lookout on the bridge!

I did shine our mega candle power searchlight onto the mainsail to give them something to see, but by then they had already started to alter course. I was grateful to them for doing the right thing – it wasn't always so! For the first time I realized *Bente* would have been better with masthead navigation lights instead of on the bow.

During my 0300 to 0500 watch the Shipwash light came into view, and toward the end I felt that the seas were lessening. We must have been coming into the lee of the coast. When Charles came up at 0500 we manoeuvered past the light vessel, close by, then threaded through several ferries and container ships from Gothenberg and Hook of Holland, converging toward the channel, and southward for Harwich.

We followed, hugging the edge of the channel, realizing that the tide would be all wrong for going into the Deben. I gratefully accepted Charles' suggestion that we go to the Shotley Point marina where his family kept their boat and they were well known.

Turing into Harwich harbour we downed sails and motored over to Shotley and were welcomed into the marina's lock at 0830.

For me the trip wouldn't be completed until *Bente* was on her mooring at Waldringfield, so Charles agreed to go home, rest, and come back by 1300 to help me go up the Deben on the last of the flood tide.

I set about bringing cushions, sails, and clothing on deck and jetty to dry in the lovely warm morning sun, in the clear skies and gentle breeze that welcomed us home.

Charles appeared on schedule, and brought his mother along with him.

This was the lady who had crossed the Atlantic two years before in the large, sturdy, family yacht, but with just Charles and his sister as crew. She was very welcome on board! We had a pleasant motor up the coast, across the bar, and up the Deben, enjoying some white wine, snacks, and exchanges of yarns.

At 1700 we picked up *Bente's* mooring, and there were my wife and younger son waving from the shore and launching the dinghy to come out to us.

Rowing away later, I looked back and *Bente* seemed to be sitting rather pertly at her mooring, as if pleased with herself.

And so she might be!

Bente arrived home with no breakage or damage beyond some scratches on the rubbing strake, and beyond the brief 'outage' on the Navstar electric circuit, there were no problems during the trip. Boat preparation is, for me, a top priority.

The time spent in passage planning during the winter was usually rewarded by being able to reach our chosen destination, or first alternative safe haven, and having the charts and information necessary to arrive safely.

As it turned out the story shows a preoccupation with the weather conditions on this trip – and so it was. Perhaps that is not unusual in what was more like 'passage making' than just 'cruising', and perhaps the extraordinarily bad weather in the summer of '93 contributed. The danger of not obtaining the best possible weather information each day of going to sea was underlined in the Kattegat, and again in the North Sea off the Frisian Islands.

I was told that the risk of gales in our cruising area in summer time is normally less than 5 percent – say 2 days in 40!

We are therefore due some very good summers ahead to regain the average.

I can't wait to go again!

Trophy presentation at Cowes, 1997

Diane

My first impulse on being asked to speak today was to say no. It is not easy to speak about personal matters of an emotional nature, especially at a public gathering. However, on reflection, I felt perhaps I had a responsibility as a new citizen of this country to share with you what it means to me.

As some of you already know, I was born and raised in Canada, and although I had been to the United States on many occasions as a visitor, it never occurred to me I might one day become a citizen. In my experience, visitors here have a relatively easy time crossing back and forth, and I took for granted many of the things which I now realize are so hard won. Like most of you, I grew up in a free country – free to vote, to travel, to study, to work, to marry, to bring up a family in my own way, and to cross the border with a minimum of red tape. We tend to forget how fortunate we are, and become complacent, and sometimes neglectful of our responsibilities as citizens.

When changes in my personal life brought me here, I took for granted that there would be no problem. I was a fortunate person making a choice between two democratic countries, and was free to make that choice. Many who apply for citizenship are fleeing from tyranny in other parts of the world, the kind of tyranny that brought the first settlers to this country hundreds of years ago.

The first six months of my stay, I was on a visitor's visa which is good for only six months. Toward the end of that time I received a notice from the Immigration Department to depart from the country. My first rude awakening! However, my marriage was pending, and I was granted a temporary extension. Right after the wedding my husband made application for my registration as a resident alien, and the fun began.

The purpose of the requirements is to protect the health, welfare and security of the United States. Therefore, it was necessary for me to have a physical exam, chest X-ray and blood test, sign affidavits to the effect that I had never been a victim of mental illness or drug addiction, never convicted of any criminal offense, never been a member of any Communist organization or any affiliated organization, able to read and write in the English language, and be financially secure. After two months of preparation of documents, and interview, I was finally given permission to live in the United States as a resident alien.

At that time I had no intention of becoming an American citizen. All my roots were in Canada, including a large family, and I had yet no awareness of the complications ahead. I learned that each year in January I must register with the Dept. of Immigration so that they could keep track of my whereabouts. My frequent visits to Canada became something more than routine checks as before. Now I had to present my alien registration card each time. Still, these restrictions were not confining, and I still had strong emotional ties to the country where I was born.

As time passed, and I began to feel more at home here, took an interest in what was going on around me, I realized I was unable to take a really active part due to my inability to vote. My husband hoped I would be able to assist him his real estate business, but discovered that one of the requirements for a broker's license was citizenship. Finally, when my Canadian passport was due to expire, I realized the time had come to make a decision.

A person must be a resident of this country for five years (three years if married to a citizen) before one is eligible to apply for citizenship. So I had already met the first requirement. Then I had to repeat in more depth the documentation of my own history and background, be fingerprinted again at our local jail, have several more identical photographs taken. I was informed I would be given an oral examination on the history, government and constitution of the United States. Not being sure how extensive that might be, I spent quite some time cramming!

I was required to bring two other persons with me that crucial day – my sponsor (my husband) and one other responsible citizen, not related to me, who had known me for at least six months. We were each interviewed separately, and you can imagine how nervewracking it was waiting out in the corridor of the Court building in Portland for my turn to come. There were numerous other people of all ages and nationalities lined up and awaiting their turn also. I was pleasantly surprised to find the officer very understanding and reassuring. After lengthy questioning, I was told I would be informed by mail of the verdict. More waiting!

Finally, on November 6th, 1978 my day arrived. As I remember there were about 300 new citizens waiting to be sworn in that day, from every country in the world. It was a very emotional day – feeling proud and humble all at the same time. There were so many relatives and friends accompanying these new citizens that many had to stand outside in the corridors, and were unable to watch the ceremony. After numerous speeches by various dignitaries the ceremony began. Due to the large number of applicants we read the Oath of Allegiance together, and I think it was then the finality of my decision struck home.

After that our names were read, one by one, and we each made our way to the platform to receive our papers, and be officially welcomed into the United States as full-fledged citizens. There were a number of ladies there, I think, representing the Daughters of the American Revolution, who also lined up to shake hands as we passed through the receiving line. They gave us each a small flag, and a pamphlet with instructions on how to display, respect, and care for the flag.

As I came out, I felt like a student on graduation day – that one era of my life had just come to an end, and a new exciting one was just beginning. I wanted everyone to know that I was finally graduated and was now officially a part of this wonderful country. The timing was just great as that day also happened to be election day, and after celebrating over a delightful lunch in Portland, I made my way to Norway Fire Station to cast my first ballot.

That was not quite the end of my excitement, for shortly afterwards, I received two unexpected letters of congratulations in the mail – one from Governor Longley, and one from Senator Edmund Muskie.

So that is why I changed my mind and decided to come here today. I feel I must do my part as a citizen of this country which holds freedom so dear. The other aspect of freedom is responsibility, and we all bear responsibility to our country to do whatever we can to protect that freedom. Until today I have remained uncommitted as far as political parties are concerned, but I can see the necessity for nominating good candidates, and I want to share in that decision making, so I intend to join the Republican Party today, if I may. Thank you.

Diane

Since attending a briefing conducted by the Department of Energy on the Nuclear Waste Depository Project in Maine, I have been feeling so angry about what is going on that I felt compelled to write to you. The DOE representatives were less than candid in their responses to our questions, and contradicted themselves numerous times, lessening their credibility, and increasing our fears about their motives. The provisions of the Nuclear Waste Policy Act of 1982, which provides for a 90 day information period, I feel were violated by them due to their inability or unwillingness to answer even the most fundamental questions relative to the project and our safety.

How can we have faith in an agency which, while charged with the task of finding a safe repository for high level nuclear waste, is simultaneously promoting the nuclear industry? In this situation can we really trust that safety is their primary concern? Could this conflict of interest disqualify the department from carrying out this task?

My objections to this project are based on a firm belief that storing nuclear waste underground *anywhere* has not been proven a safe option. To consider underground storage in an area of Maine which is riddled with lakes and streams, which supplies water for the most heavily populated area in the State, and which is located along a geologic fault line is incredible!

The storage of other hazardous materials underground has already had serious effects on water supplies. Leakage from underground gasoline storage tanks, leaching of dioxin from toxic waste dumps, and radioactive contamination from other nuclear installations should be sufficient evidence that we are not technologically ready to ensure the safety of such an undertaking here.

To spend several years exploring the feasibility of this project, using up to 10 metric tons of high level nuclear waste to test the site, will sentence this area to death, whether or not the permanent storage is approved. Our economy will suffer irreparable damage just from the possibility of this occurring here.

I am convinced that this site will ultimately be ruled out for technical reasons. Nevertheless, I beg you to exert all possible effort and influence to have the Nuclear Waste Policy of 1982 repealed or amended so that we may pursue research to find a more acceptable solution for the permanent disposal of nuclear waste. Unless that is done, I feel we should shut down all nuclear plants until a satisfactory and safe way *is* found.

Tess

Every Person in the world has memories that they treasure. Within families there are common memories that they all share. Some memories are held close and others drift with time. I chose to draw this picture because of the people in it. They link this family together. They link me to you. My lifetime has only been 16 years and I already have so many memories. Some are good, and some are bad. But I find that if we cling to the good ones and take what we get out of the bad ones, we become better people in the end. I remember so many things about the many visits to Maine. Our Christmases in July, our swims across the lake and feeding the geese are things that I thought that everyone would write about. But I remember so much more than that. I remember the little things too. I have faint images in my head of how I think of you. You were always the person who made the best cookies, read the best stories, take us on great adventure through the woods and push other people to please us. Grampa Ed was always the big teddy bear. I remember the old screened-in porch with the picnic table. He would go out there in the morning with Brooke and I, when no one else was up. He would take us water skiing, and let us drive the boat when we went for our many boat rides at sunset. The dragon we rode on, the puzzles, scrabble, reading in the hammock and eating those famous treats you made were good memories too. I remember the room that Brooke and I stayed in really quite well. It had 2 single beds (which we were very thankful for), the curtains with hanging pom poms, and the closet door with all of our measurements on it. I was always so pleased when I grew because it meant that I was getting older and I was catching up with Brooke. (Which never quite seemed to happen.) Then there are the special things that I remember about the town. Every time we drove through the main stretch of Norway, I had a little ritual (which I never knew I had until now). I would realize we were in Norway from the church bell. Then we would pass the Jack and Jill store, Ames, the great ice cream place and this one special with a wooden canoe. It's funny, the things that I remember. My mom still laughs every time she sees the picture with Brooke and I eating marshmallows and I am completely naked except for 2 Band-Aids on each of my knees. I also remember Grampa Ed's tractor thingy. I never knew what that was called. Come to think of it, I still don't. I loved that. Not necessarily to ride it, but just sitting in it made me feel so special, so grown up. My dad always thought of those things as his toys. He still does – I guess some things never change. Heehee! So I wanted to wish you a VERY Happy Birthday. I hope you liked your drawing.

David

Watching

While watching the time,
Watching it go by.

While watching the time fly by,
I watch one of nature's
Most beautiful creations,
The Clouds.

While watching time go by,
I see the clouds take their shape,
Their form.

While watching the clouds,
I see what I have never seen
Before ……

Tapestry: Thick hand-woven fabric with a pictorial or ornamental design formed by the weft-threads.

Warp: Threads stretched lengthwise in loom to be crossed by weft.

Weft: Threads crossing from side to side of web and interweaving with warp.

Reader's Digest
Encyclopedic Dictionary
compiled by Oxford University Press
Oxford, Eng. 1962

Contributors

Doctor Thomas Bartow, an elderly clergyman and U.K. ancestor.

Mary Elisabeth Young Hammer, a young wife and businesswoman, my daughter.

Edith Heard, a middle-aged tenant farmer, a U.K. relative.

Mr. Melhuish, a farm owner, a U.K. ancestor.

Frederick and Laura Melhuish, Ontario relatives.

David Maxwell Roberston, an elementary school student, my nephew.

Dorothy Isabel Scott Robertson, a high school student, my mother.

Ross Ian Robertson, a business executive, husband and father, my younger brother.

Ross Maxwell Robertson, a young businessman, husband and father, my father.

Taun Maxwell Robertson, a retired businessman, husband and father, my youngest brother.

Diane Adele Robertson, a public health nurse, wife 1) Walter, 2) Travis, and mother, my sister.

Tess Walter, a high school student, my sister's granddaughter.

Barbara Joan Robertson Young, a retired university employee, ex-wife and mother.

Acknowledgements

I couldn't have continued with my work this year without the help of many people.

Each played a different but significant role and my grateful thanks goes to Willie Ducross, Beverly Robert, Taun and Trudy Robertson, Lise Vigneault, Mouna Shawa, June Hussey, Lydia Quarty, and James, John and Angie Dos Santos. Their tender concern gave me the strength to carry on in spite of personal woes.

Mary Plawutsky of the Quebec Family History Society and Kathryn Reed were kind enough to answer my calls for typists.

Mouna Shawa designed the tapestry for the cover.

B JAQUES77